CAMPAIGN • 243

THE FALL OF THE PHILIPPINES 1941–42

CLAYTON CHUN　　ILLUSTRATED BY HOWARD GERRARD

Series editor Marcus Cowper

First published in Great Britain in 2012 by Osprey Publishing,
PO Box 883, Oxford, OX1 9PL, UK
PO Box 3985, New York, NY 10185-3985, USA
Email: info@ospreypublishing.com

Osprey Publishing, part of Bloomsbury Publishing Plc

Transferred to digital print on demand 2016.

First published 2012
2nd impression 2012

Printed and bound by Cadmus Communications, USA

A CIP catalogue record for this book is available from the
British Library.

ISBN: 978 1 84908 609 7
PDF e-book ISBN: 978 1 84908 610 3
EPUB e-book ISBN: 978 1 78096 392 1

Editorial by Ilios Publishing Ltd, Oxford, UK
(www.iliospublishing.com)
Page layout by The Black Spot
Index by Sandra Shotter
Typeset in Sabon and Myriad Pro
Maps by Bounford.com
3D bird's-eye view by The Black Spot
Battlescene illustrations by Howard Gerrard
Originated by Blenheim Colour Ltd

Dedication

To those who fought for freedom in the Philippines.

Acknowledgements

I want to thank Mr. Marcus Cowper for all of the gracious
help and support to make this project come through. The US
Army War College, especially the Dean of Academics Dr.
William Johnsen, also allowed me the time to research and
complete this book. Finally, my family gave me much
encouragement to write.

Artist's note

Readers may care to note that the original paintings from which
the color plates in this book were prepared are available for
private sale. The Publishers retain all reproduction copyright
whatsoever. All inquiries should be addressed to:

Howard Gerrard, 11 Oaks Road, Tenterden, TN30 6RD, UK

The Publishers regret that they can enter into no
correspondence upon this matter.

Glossary

AAA	antiaircraft artillery
AAF	Army Air Forces
FEAF	Far East Air Force
IGHQ	Imperial General Headquarters
IJA	Imperial Japanese Army
IJAAF	Imperial Japanese Army Air Force
IJN	Imperial Japanese Navy
IJNAF	Imperial Japanese Navy Air Force
PA	Philippine Army
PS	Philippine Scouts
PT	patrol torpedo
USAAFE	United States Army Forces in the Far East
USFIP	United States Forces in the Philippines
WPO	War Plan Orange

The Woodland Trust

Osprey Publishing are supporting the Woodland Trust, the UK's
leading woodland conservation charity, by funding the
dedication of trees.

www.ospreypublishing.com

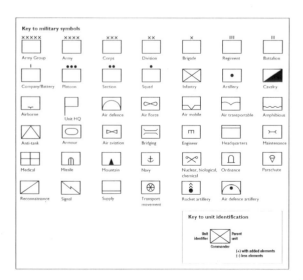

CONTENTS

Japanese plans for Pacific Area operations

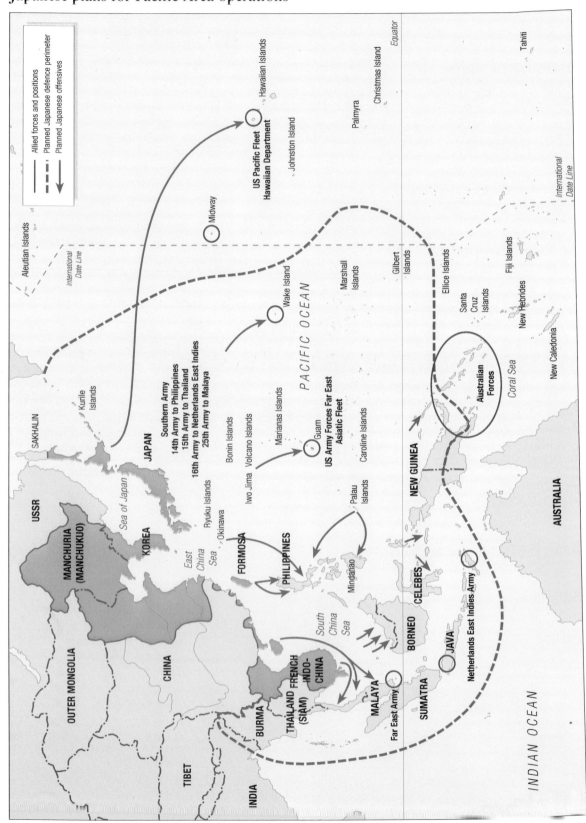

INTRODUCTION

The Japanese conquest of the Philippines was one of largest losses for the United States early in World War II. The Pearl Harbor attack frequently overshadows the campaign in the Philippines archipelago that started on December 8, 1941 and lasted six months. Perhaps due to the sudden, massive Japanese aircraft carrier strike, in the minds of many the Pearl Harbor attack became a more devastating military event than the seizure of the Philippines. Both Hawaii and the Philippines were under American control, one a territory and the other a commonwealth. The Pacific Fleet had suffered major losses and the Hawaiian Air Force had its airfields ravaged by Japanese aircraft. In the Philippines, the Japanese invaded and took control of the land and its people. An American Army division was lost, the Asiatic Fleet retreated out of the Philippines, and the bomber and fighter force were destroyed. In terms of casualties and scope of combat, the Philippines represented a much larger defeat. Still, the dogged American-Filipino defense of the islands provided a flicker of light in the darkest days for Washington in World War II.

JAPAN AND THE UNITED STATES: OPPOSING POWERS IN THE PACIFIC

Imperial Japan entered the 20th century with a great demonstration of its budding national power. Much of that national power centered on its expanding military capability. Japan had participated in quelling the 1900–

This Japanese depiction of the Pearl Harbor attack illustrates the meticulous planning and operational capability that Tokyo used to conduct near-simultaneous operations throughout the Pacific. The Japanese hoped to destroy the US Pacific Fleet. (US Army)

01 Boxer Rebellion that cemented its commercial and political interests in China. Its victory over Russia in 1905 led to additional respect for the Japanese and transferred Korea to its regional sphere of influence. Russia was a relatively weak nation, but this was the first instance that a modern Asian country had defeated a European one. Next, Tokyo joined the Allies against Imperial Germany during World War I and took over its territories and interests in China and several Pacific island groups. Japanese political, economic, and military influence widened. Tokyo's imperial growth was a function of its burgeoning industry – Japan's factories required an expanded source and market for raw materials, which the home islands lacked. If resources became limited, Japan's desire to become the dominant power in the Far East and the Pacific would end prematurely.

Washington had a different dilemma in the Pacific, with its focus on leaving the Philippines. The US took control over the Philippines during the 1898 Spanish-American War. Spain ceded her former colony, for $20 million, as a part of the Treaty of Paris. Washington fought and defeated a bloody Philippine Insurrection from 1899 to 1902 as insurgents sought immediate independence for the native Filipinos. Some Filipinos believed that they had merely traded their Spanish occupiers for American ones; while American opponents to the acquisition of the Philippines had decried the annexation as raw colonialism. By 1916 Washington promised self-government to the Filipinos, with the US government hoping to prepare the Philippines for full independence. The Commonwealth of the Philippines looked forward to that event with the passing of the Tydings-McDuffie Act in 1934 that promised freedom by 1946. These events had colored American military planning on the value of the islands to American interests in the Pacific and Asia. Japan's demand for resources and America's ambivalence about the Philippines formed the backdrop as both countries collided over Tokyo's rise in Asia and the Pacific.

JAPANESE INTERESTS AND MOTIVATIONS FOR WAR

China was the scene of Japanese territorial advances throughout the 1920s and 1930s. Each advance into Manchuria and later China was punctuated by denunciations from the League of Nations and others, including the United States, who deplored Tokyo's unabashed seizure of lands and outrages against civilians. However, the war in China, for the Japanese, became one of attrition that did not lead to a clear-cut victory for Tokyo. Despite their advances, the Japanese were being bogged down in China and sought ways to isolate the Chinese Nationalist and Communist resistance, with attention focusing on their meager supply routes through Burma and French Indochina.

Japan forced a weakened Vichy French government to allow it to occupy Indochina on September 2, 1940, under strong protests from Washington. This occupation allowed Tokyo to shut down two Chinese supply routes from French territory. Earlier, on July 18, Prime Minister Winston Churchill closed the Burma Road to traffic under pressure from the Japanese. Churchill later reopened the road on October 18. Washington took a more active role to counter the Japanese, and instituted an American steel embargo against Tokyo on September 26. The embargo was a direct result of the Japanese occupation of Indochina and the threat to China and Southeast Asia that it represented. Washington also increased aid to the Nationalist Chinese forces. Later, Washington froze Japanese assets in the United States and stopped oil

Tokyo had to plan and execute a near-simultaneous attack against mostly British and American military forces on December 7/8, 1941. Here a Japanese aircraft carrier prepares its planes to launch an attack against American naval, military, and air bases across Hawaii. (DOD)

sales as Japanese forces expanded their seizures in Indochina. Britain followed suit as the Japanese move south was uncomfortably close to its colonial possessions of Malaya and Singapore. Japan's economy was now in danger of being starved of the resources it needed to survive.

However, the region offered plenty of resources that Tokyo could exploit. The Southeast Asian colonial possessions of Malaya and the Netherlands East Indies possessed a wealth of resources in terms of oil, metals, food, and lumber. The only obstacles for the Japanese in getting hold of these were the British in Malaya, Dutch forces in the East Indies, and Americans in the Philippines.

The Japanese government had felt constrained by the United States and other powers in the past about their expansion. The Washington, London, and Five-Power naval treaties and conferences blocked Japan's maritime growth, attempting to limit the size of the Japanese Navy to that of a second-class power. Tokyo had also recently signed a non-aggression pact with Moscow. Since the 1905 war, both powers had skirmished over borders in Mongolia and Soviet forces had demonstrated their abilities to best the Japanese at the Khalkin-Gol River between Mongolia and Manchuria in 1939. This non-aggression pact led to a degree of assurance in Tokyo about the possibility of a sudden Soviet attack, but Moscow still represented a threat. Now, America and Britain were attempting to strangle the Japanese economy through sanctions. Without raw materials and capital resources the Japanese economy would falter, and Tokyo's ability to maintain its empire would wither away. The Western powers had the ability to transform Japan back to a small power.

Tokyo still had an opportunity to escape this perceived threat. With France and the Netherlands defeated in Europe, Tokyo had to take action, whether by diplomatic or military means, to gain assured access to raw materials. Japanese forces were already in Indochina. Britain was under attack by Germany. However, in September 1940 Japan failed to get the Netherlands East Indies to guarantee the equivalent of the nation's annual oil requirements. Tokyo tried diplomatic means through negotiations with Washington, but did not succeed in having the embargoes withdrawn. Military intervention now seemed a realistic option for Tokyo.

The US entered the War with Spain in 1898 and ended with several possessions in the Pacific, like the Philippines. Here, the 51st Iowa Volunteer Infantry Regiment departs the Presidio of San Francisco for occupation duty in Manila in 1898. (US Army)

THE PHILIPPINES: AMERICA'S FAR EASTERN OUTPOST

The Philippines represented an important part of Washington's strategy in the Pacific and Far East. American commanders could use its military presence to deter potential aggression by Japan and, if necessary, as a springboard for launching an attack. The Philippines was much closer to Tokyo than Hawaii or the West Coast of the United States, and the air, land, and naval forces in the Philippines represented the spear point of Washington's reach into Asia. This outpost represented a huge military commitment with naval facilities, large numbers of modern fighters and bombers, an American Army division, massive coastal and harbor defenses, and its commitment to train a huge Philippine Army (PA) composed largely of reservists. The American forces, along with the British in Malaya and Singapore, represented a direct military threat to the designs of the Japanese in their quest for resources in Southeast Asia. Still, life among the Americans in the Philippines seemed uneventful in the pre-war days. Duty was easy for the American military personnel assigned to the islands. Washington was transforming their colony into a democracy, but it would take time.

Some in Washington believed that the Philippines did not represent an object of great strategic value. They believed that the Philippines, with over 7,000 islands, was indefensible. It contained few natural resources. The major base for the US Navy was in Subic Bay, but it too was difficult to defend. American troops and regular PA units were few in number given the responsibility of defending such a large area. However, Japanese advances throughout Asia and the Pacific, plus the elevation of Douglas MacArthur as commander of American and PA units, convinced many in the War Department that a defense of the archipelago was possible. Instead of keeping a minimum of forces, the War Department expanded the American commitment to the Philippines with additional weapons, forces, and promises of more help. The Philippines campaign would provide the first sustained operation against Japan in a long and bloody war.

CHRONOLOGY

1941

December 8

0230hrs — Asiatic Fleet Headquarters receives radio transmission about the Pearl Harbor attack. The Philippines is 18 hours ahead of Hawaii.

0400hrs — IJNAF aircraft launch from the *Ryujo* to attack Davao.

0500hrs — Brereton attempts to secure MacArthur's approval for launching a B-17 attack on Japanese bases on Formosa. Sutherland tells Brereton that MacArthur does not have time to see him.

0530hrs — Washington contacts MacArthur about the Pearl Harbor strike and tells him to execute Rainbow-5.

0700hrs — Fog clears over Formosa, which had delayed an earlier launch of IJAAF and IJNAF aircraft, allowing attack forces to leave their bases. All aircraft get in the air by 0845hrs.

0800hrs — Brereton orders B-17s at Clark to conduct aerial patrols to watch for an invasion fleet, Japanese aircraft, and avoid an air attack while on the ground.

0900hrs — Brereton receives reports of airborne Japanese bombers heading south. He launches his B-17s in Luzon to avoid the Japanese catching them on the ground.

0930hrs — IJAAF aircraft hit Baguio and Tuguegarao.

1235hrs — IJNAF aircraft smash Iba.

1240hrs — Japanese aircraft bomb and strafe Clark Field.

Japanese take Bataan Island.

December 10 — IJA forces land at Aparri and Vigan. Japanese aircraft destroy Cavite and airfields around Manila.

December 12 — Japanese forces come ashore at Legaspi.

December 17 — Remaining B-17s in Del Monte leave for Australia.

December 22 — Japanese forces invade the Lingayen Gulf.

December 24 — MacArthur changes strategy and implements WPO-3. IJA units land at Lamon Bay. For the next week, Wainwright's forces forestall the Japanese offensive through the Central Luzon Plain and start delaying actions against the 48th Division moving south.

December, 26 — Manila declared an "open city."

December, 31 — McArthur withdraws all forces out of Manila.

1942

January 1	Jones' forces retreat across the Calumpit bridges.
January 5	American-Filipino ground forces put on half-rations.
January 7	Remaining units in central Luzon move into Bataan.
January 9	Nara initiates attack on the Abucay Line.
January 10	MacArthur travels to Bataan from Corregidor.
January 15	The 51st Division moves back under Japanese pressure in the Abucay Line's western sector.
January 16	Japanese forces reach Moron.
January 21	The Kimura Detachment and 20th Infantry Regiment break through the Mauban Line to the West Road.
January 22	MacArthur decides to abandon the main battle positions.
January 26	American and Filipino units establish themselves into the Bagac–Orion Line.
January 23	Japanese units conduct an amphibious operation to deploy troops behind the Bagac–Orion Line. This begins the "Battle of the Points."
January 28	Nara penetrates the Bagac–Orion Line, but the defenders do not break.
January 29	Japanese units destroyed at Longoskawayan Point.

February 8	American forces, using their own amphibious attack, try to evict the remaining Japanese forces at Quinauan Point. Nara disengages from the Bagac–Orion Line.
February 10	Homma requests reinforcements to conquer Bataan.
February 22	Roosevelt orders MacArthur out of the Philippines to Australia.
March 12	MacArthur leaves Corregidor.
April 3	Homma's heavy artillery begins bombardment against the American-Filipino defenders.
April 9	Japanese forces require only a day to smash the Bagac–Orion Line. King surrenders Bataan.
April 10	The IJA invades Cebu.
April 29	The Kawaguchi Detachment lands on Mindanao and begins campaign to defeat the last major Filipino outposts in the southern Philippines.
May 5	Japanese landing craft transports troops to Corregidor. Wainwright surrenders the island.
May 6	Wainwright assumes command of all forces in the Philippines and surrenders unconditionally his entire command to Homma.
June 9	All organized resistance ceases in the Philippines.

OPPOSING COMMANDERS

American and Japanese commanders mostly fought the Philippines campaign. American Army officers largely led the effort to defend the Philippines. Although the majority of military personnel were Filipinos, American officers had taken over training and command of most of the PA divisions throughout the fight. Japanese commanders fighting in the Philippines were primarily from the Imperial Japanese Army (IJA) who had to conquer and occupy the Pacific archipelago. Although the Japanese used naval forces, their mission involved transporting troops for invasion, conducting air operations or protecting sea lines of communications.

US COMMANDERS

Lieutenant General Douglas MacArthur, commander of US Army Forces in the Far East (USAFFE), commanded all ground and air forces in the Philippines. This included American and Philippine Army units. Son of Medal of Honor winner Lieutenant General Arthur MacArthur, he served his first assignment as an engineer in the Philippines after graduation from West Point in 1903. MacArthur's father had been military governor of the Philippines in 1900. He became the youngest brigadier general of the American Expeditionary Force in World War I; Superintendent of the US Military Academy; Commander, Military District of Manila; Chief of Staff of the Army; and, after retirement, military adviser to Philippine President Manuel Quezon. President Franklin Roosevelt had recalled MacArthur to active duty in 1941 to command the American Army and PA. As USAFFE's commander, MacArthur controlled ground and air forces to defend the islands. There was no single commander of all military forces in the Philippines and MacArthur did not have control of naval forces. This lack of organization would create unity of command issues later in the campaign.

As the Japanese overcame American-Filipino opposition, Roosevelt ordered MacArthur to leave the Philippines to become Commander-in-Chief, Southwest Pacific Area, in Australia. MacArthur's forces fought a tough campaign in New Guinea and throughout the Southwest Pacific area. He would later lead American forces in the retaking of the Philippines and serve as the Supreme Commander for the Allied Powers leading the planned invasion and occupation of Japan. MacArthur accepted the surrender of Japan in Tokyo Bay on September 2, 1945. During his command in the Philippines, questions arose about his strategy; the destruction of his air forces

on the ground; a payment of $500,000 by Quezon for services as military adviser; statements to his Bataan defenders about reinforcements that never came; and only visiting soldiers fighting on Bataan once while staying on Corregidor. Despite these concerns, Roosevelt promoted him to General of the Army in December 1944. MacArthur also had a difficult and strained relationship with one of his staff officers in the pre-war years in the Philippines, Dwight Eisenhower. Eisenhower had served as his chief of staff and frequently disagreed with MacArthur over strategy, policy, and the training of the Philippine military. He left MacArthur in 1940.

MacArthur's Army Air Forces (AAF) commander was **Major General Lewis Brereton**. Brereton came to MacArthur's staff in November 1941 to become commander of the Far East Air Force (FEAF). MacArthur had fired his predecessor and looked to Brereton to improve the FEAF. Under his direction, the FEAF was expanded with additional aircraft and air base construction. His role in the destruction of much of the FEAF on the ground hours after the attack on Pearl Harbor has been the subject of much historical debate and, like his predecessor, he was sacked by MacArthur, having been transferred to Australia midway through the campaign. Brereton would later take charge of the Ninth Air Force and conduct the ineffective and costly Ploesti oil field raids. However, he did provide valued close air support and interdiction during the Normandy campaign. Brereton also commanded the First Allied Airborne Army during Operations *Market-Garden* and *Varsity*. Allegations of dereliction of duty over the FEAF's destruction followed Brereton after the war.

MacArthur divided his USAFFE ground units into three major geographic forces. **Major General Jonathan Wainwright**, a career cavalryman, directed the North Luzon Force, responsible for areas north of Manila. Wainwright had graduated from the US Military Academy in 1902. He worked on war plans for the Philippines as a General Staff officer in the War Department and was also the commander of the US Army's Philippine Division before the war. MacArthur appointed Wainwright in charge of forces on Bataan and Corregidor when he left for Australia. General George C. Marshall, Chief of Staff of the Army, had suggested to Roosevelt that Wainwright receive the Congressional Medal of Honor for his defense of Bataan and Corregidor against overwhelming odds. MacArthur vehemently disagreed and fought the award, claiming that Wainwright had surrendered his forces without approval and had led his troops poorly. Wainwright would endure more than three years of brutal captivity, but he would be on the USS *Missouri* in Tokyo Bay to witness the Japanese surrender. After his release from a Japanese POW camp, he had been concerned that the Army would court martial him for his surrender of the Philippines. Instead, President Harry Truman promoted him to full general and nominated Wainwright for the Medal of Honor, which he received.

Controlling the South Luzon Force was **Major General George Parker Jr**. Once MacArthur decided to move to Bataan as the final defense position on Luzon, Parker became Commander, Bataan Defense Force. He would later serve as II Philippine Corps commander facing the brunt of Japanese efforts to break through in Bataan. Parker survived imprisonment in Formosa during the war.

Brigadier General William Sharp was responsible for the defense of the Visayan–Mindanao area. Sharp's forces were the last to surrender and Wainwright had to convince his American-Filipino forces to do so. Many did not, for fear of mistreatment by the Japanese and their continued ability to resist. These forces became guerillas and harassed the IJA throughout the war. MacArthur, before leaving the Philippines, had ordered Sharp to wage a guerilla war in Mindanao if Bataan and Corregidor surrendered.

General Homma Masaharu was commander of the 14th Army, responsible for the Philippines campaign. He suffered great humiliation during the campaign due to his failure to capture the Philippines on schedule. Washington later tried him as a war criminal. (US Army)

Admiral Thomas C. Hart served as Commander-in-Chief Asiatic Fleet. Hart, in poor health, had a stormy relationship with MacArthur. Differences in strategy prompted MacArthur and Hart to clash and, although Hart and MacArthur lived in the same Manila hotel, they seldom coordinated on war planning or strategy. Even after the beginning of hostilities MacArthur failed to inform Hart of his actions. For example, MacArthur did not inform Hart of his declaration to make Manila an open city beforehand. Additionally, Hart outranked MacArthur despite the size of the land forces in the Philippines relative to the smaller US Navy. MacArthur characterized Hart as "Big Admiral, Small Fleet." MacArthur believed that the Navy's plan to move south of Luzon during any Japanese attack on the Philippines was tantamount to surrender. Although Hart tried to support a more active defense of the Philippines, the Navy Department overruled him. His submarine and limited surface forces tried to oppose the Japanese invasion fleets, but they were overwhelmed. The admiral would later command the American British Dutch Australian naval forces, but his forces could not stop the Imperial Japanese Navy (IJN) in their offensive against the Netherlands East Indies. Hart returned to the United States and retired in July 1942.

JAPANESE COMMANDERS

Lieutenant General Homma Masaharu was commander of the IJA's 14th Army responsible for the invasion and occupation of the Philippines. He came on active army service after graduation from the IJA's military academy in 1907. Homma saw service in France in 1918 as an observer to the British Expeditionary Force. He later served as military attaché in Britain in 1930. As a divisional commander, Homma experienced combat in China in 1939. Homma came under heavy criticism by the Imperial General Headquarters (IGHQ) for his lack of progress in the conquest of the Philippines. He would retire early in August 1943. Despite the conduct of his troops in the Bataan Death March, he had ordered his troops to treat the Filipinos with respect and not conduct crimes against them in order to ease the occupation. After the war, an American war crimes tribunal tried Homma for IJA atrocities, including the Bataan Death March. MacArthur signed his death warrant and Homma died by firing squad in 1946.

Lieutenant General Nara Akira, commander of the 65th Independent Mixed Brigade, was familiar with the US Army. He had graduated from the US Army Infantry School in 1927. Homma had slated the 65th Brigade, formed in 1941 at Hiroshima, for garrison duty after the fall of the Philippines, but Nara would have to command his forces in combat in Bataan and try to defeat a dug-in force. Nara's failure to defeat the American-Filipino forces in Bataan forced Homma to relieve him from operations against the I Corps area.

OPPOSING FORCES

Japanese ground, air, and naval forces had a major challenge to defeat a relatively large USAFFE force. The Philippines garrison represented the second biggest concentration of American Army forces in the Pacific next to Hawaii. The bulk of the ground opposition facing the Japanese was the PA. Although the PA had thousands of troops, it lacked modern weapons, training, equipment, and experienced commissioned and non-commissioned officers. MacArthur's immediate goal was getting these divisions prepared to confront an experienced invader. He also placed great faith in a possible equalizer, the airplane. MacArthur had been convinced that advanced B-17 bombers and fighter aircraft could compensate for his lack of trained and equipped ground forces. As a result, MacArthur and some Army war planners had persuaded the president, Marshall, and other military leaders to expand reinforcements to include additional aircraft, American soldiers, and equipment. This would require time. The US Navy's Asiatic Fleet also maintained a forward presence in the region. For Hart, the Asiatic Fleet depended on a few cruisers and World War I-vintage destroyers. The Navy did have many submarines, but it could not contest the Japanese control of the sea. Despite these actions, the US was not ready for combat operations in December 1941.

The AAF did not have many modern B-17 aircraft just before the war. Arnold sent most of the B-17 AAF fleet to the Philippines and Hawaii. This B-17C represented a technological marvel at the time, but did not provide a significant role in the Philippines other than being a major target for Japanese aircraft. (US Air Force)

The Japanese also had significant forces in the area. The Japanese Southern Expeditionary Army, with headquarters in Saigon, French Indochina, had control of four numbered armies, including the 14th designated for the Philippines operation. In contrast to Washington's military units, Tokyo had mobilized most of its military forces and many of its soldiers had tasted combat in China and Manchuria. However, they faced a different problem: the Japanese could not concentrate solely on the Philippines as they also had plans to take action around the Pacific, Southeast Asia, and other targets in Asia. IJA aircraft also supported strategic bombing, close air support, and interdiction missions.

The IJN, under the Combined Fleet, also devoted considerable forces against not only the Philippines, but against Hawaii, Wake Island, Malaya, the Netherlands East Indies, Hong Kong, and other targets. Japanese naval aircraft would play a vital, early role in Tokyo's plans to win the Philippines; much like it relied on this arm at Pearl Harbor.

US AND PHILIPPINE FORCES

The American Army had 22,532 personnel in the Philippines just before hostilities with Japan broke out. Most of the USAFFE consisted of infantrymen, approximately 7,300 personnel. Half of the USAFFE consisted of Philippine Scouts (PS). Well trained, motivated, and officered, the PS provided some of MacArthur's best combat capabilities in terms of disciplined fighting power. Another large contingent was the American coastal defense artillery units used to guard fortifications that protected Manila and Subic Bays. The coastal defense units typically operated high-caliber howitzers and mortars to sink enemy naval vessels. These units also provided some antiaircraft artillery (AAA) to defend selected airfields and cities.

The largest American ground force was in the Philippine Division. Headquartered at Fort William McKinley outside of Manila, the USAFFE stationed the division's three regiments and support units throughout the Philippines. The only "all" American regiment was the 31st Infantry, the other two were the 45th and 57th Infantry made up of PS personnel.

The FEAF deployed the majority of its B-17 fleet to the Philippines to bolster its fighting forces. This B-17D was very different to the aircraft used in the Combined Bomber Offensive over Germany. For example, it had fewer defensive guns. (US Air Force)

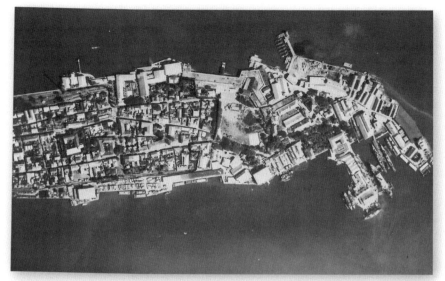

Although Filipino, they enlisted for service in the US Army. The Philippine Division did not have any organic armor. Another PS unit was the 26th Cavalry, a horse-mounted unit that contained some armored scout cars. This unit only had two squadrons, but it would see extensive combat in Luzon and Bataan. Other PS organizations consisted of two field artillery regiments.

Marshall, based on a War Plans Division study, had recommended that MacArthur receive almost all of his requested aid and reinforcements. This was no small undertaking. The pre-war Army did not have the funds, personnel, equipment, and industrial capacity to reinforce the Philippines. Another obstacle was how to ship sufficient aid to the Philippines. The lack of Navy transportation and escorts limited the amount of men and equipment sent to MacArthur. At the same time, Washington was sending war materials via the Merchant Marine, supported by the Navy, to Britain. A "hot" war in the Atlantic against the U-boats also consumed naval assets. Additionally, MacArthur was not the only commander asking for more men, equipment, and supplies.

As war clouds gathered in the Pacific, the defense of American positions in the Philippines, Hawaii, and other garrisons took on more gravity. On August 16, MacArthur received word that Washington would start shipping reinforcements no later than September 5. This included the 200th Coastal Artillery Regiment for AAA support, a tank battalion, and an ordnance battalion. Later that month, the War Department sent additional reinforcements including another tank battalion and more self-propelled, 75mm M1897A4 gun Motor Carriage M3 halftracks capable of providing direct fire support and armor-piercing capability. The 192nd and 194th Tank Battalions came from Army National Guard units and formed the Provisional Tank Group. Armed with M3 Stuart light tanks, these crews and vehicles would provide an invaluable force to counter Japanese attacks and act as a covering force. The tanks only had 37mm guns, but against lightly armored Japanese tanks they were very effective. MacArthur could count on getting 108 M-3 Stuarts and some M3 75mm M3 halftracks. Marshall had asked if MacArthur needed another American division, most likely a National Guard infantry one, but the USAFFE commander declined. He believed that his mobilized Filipinos would suffice.

The FEAF represented a small, but growing component of the USAFFE. MacArthur had hoped to use air power to stem the Japanese masses and by December 8, the FEAF had a sizeable force. In July 1941, Major General

Henry "Hap" Arnold, chief of the Army Air Forces, had proposed an FEAF composed of 272 aircraft made up of four B-17 bombardment groups (with 68 reserve planes) and 260 fighters in two pursuit groups. Washington was sending most of its existing B-17 force in the United States to the Philippines as a deterrent against a Japanese invasion. The V Bomber Command contained the 19th Bombardment Group with four bomb squadrons of eight B-17C/D models each. The 28th and 30th Bomb Squadrons flew out of Clark Field, the largest FEAF airfield. The 14th and 93rd Bomb Squadrons operated from Del Monte. MacArthur could use these aircraft to strike at any invasion fleet or Japanese bases in Formosa.

MacArthur could call on Curtiss P-40s and obsolete Seversky P-35A fighters to protect the FEAF bases and other locations. The V Interceptor Command had already started to build up to Arnold's proposed strength with the 24th (3rd, 17th, and 20th Pursuit Squadrons) and 35th Pursuit Groups (21st and 34th Pursuit Squadrons, the group's headquarters had not arrived). These fighters staged out of Iba, Nichols, Clark, and Del Carmen Fields. The FEAF also had a number of obsolete bombers, observation, transport, and trainer aircraft. The total strength on December 1 was about 277 aircraft. Brereton had 107 (some accounts note 105 aircraft) P-40B/Es, 52 P-35As, and 35 B-17C/Ds. Arnold had assigned more P-40Es and 52 A-24 dive-bombers (based on the Navy's SBD Dauntless aircraft) for MacArthur, but most did not reach the Philippines before the war.

Japanese soldiers had endured several years of combat. On December 7, 1941, these soldiers would fight the Americans, British, and Dutch. The Japanese would prove a tough foe throughout the Pacific early in the campaign. (US Army)

MacArthur could also call on a numerically large, untested PA to protect the islands. He had envisioned the future PA force structure based largely on a small professional army that would use mobilized reservists, much like Switzerland. He did not want the future Philippine government burdened with a costly, regular military force. However, as Japan became a threat, MacArthur had to start mobilizing all of his forces. He selected September 1 as a start date for mobilizing ten PA reserve divisions. These Filipino units lacked basic training facilities, modern equipment, uniforms, rations, and other material issues. Due to these resource constraints, American officers would have to extend call-ups of the PA divisions through December 15. American officers began to train and supply these units, but they encountered many problems. With the single regular PA division, the estimated total PA strength was about 120,000 men. Most of the Filipino commissioned and non-commissioned officers in the PA divisions needed proper training and experience. Language was another issue. The Philippines was home to several dialects and many units could not communicate between themselves and their officers. Many Filipino soldiers also lacked basic education. The PA required trained leadership fighting the Japanese and many American officers had to assume command of battalions and higher formations as the war continued.

MacArthur also wanted the PA to have its own air force and the PA Air Corps was a burgeoning force. AAF officers and enlisted personnel would have to train all of the Filipino Air Corps personnel to conduct missions from reconnaissance, bombing, and fighter operations, but this was a slow process given the needs of the FEAF and limited resources. This force had about 100 pilots and 40 aircraft in 1940. By August 1941, the growing PA Air Corps had

about 500 personnel organized into six squadrons. As Washington replaced obsolete FEAF aircraft types with B-17s and P-40s, MacArthur transferred many obsolete ones, including B-10s and P-26As, to the Filipinos. The flying squadrons included observation, training, photographic, bombardment-attack, and pursuit. Most of these squadrons had few aircraft. The 6th Pursuit Squadron was the only operational fighting one and had a complement of 12 Boeing P-26As at Batangas in South Luzon.

The Asiatic Fleet was the major American naval force in the Philippines. Based at Manila, the command had responsibility for operations in the Philippines and notably China. The Navy also had a major base at Olongapo in Subic Bay. Its major logistical center was the Cavite Navy Yard. The forces around the Philippines on December 8 included the fleet's flagship, the USS *Houston*, a heavy cruiser. Hart could also deploy a light cruiser (USS *Marblehead*), World War I-era destroyers, submarines, gunboats, and support ships. The Navy also had Motor Torpedo Squadron 3 consisting of six patrol torpedo (PT) boats. The Asiatic Fleet also had patrol aircraft with Patrol Wing 10 consisting of 24 PBY Catalinas and four seaplane tenders. The Navy had a number of observation aircraft, but no fighters or attack planes. Under the Asiatic Fleet was the 4th Marine Regiment based in Shanghai, China. On December 8, most of the destroyers and the USS *Marblehead* had deployed to Borneo.

IMPERIAL JAPANESE FORCES

The IGHQ designated the 14th Army, based in Formosa, as the spearhead of the ground attack on the Philippines. As part of the IJA's Southern Expeditionary Army, the 14th Army had a force of two divisions (the 16th and 48th) and a brigade, the 65th Independent Mixed Brigade, a garrison unit. The two divisions and brigade were infantry units, with each division containing about 20,000 personnel. Homma also had access to two tank regiments, two regiments and a battalion of medium artillery, three engineer regiments, and five AAA battalions, as well as other support units. The 16th Division, which would fight the entire campaign, had served in Manchuria and fought in Northern China from 1937 to 1939, but had a mixed combat record. This division contained the 9th, 20th, and 33rd Infantry Regiments. The 48th Division had a Formosan mixed brigade (with the 1st and 2nd Formosa Infantry Regiments) and the veteran 47th Infantry Regiment, with China experience. Each of the divisions also had organic cavalry or reconnaissance, transport, artillery, and engineer regiments.

The Imperial Japanese Army Air Force (IJAAF) contributed the 5th Army Air Force Division to the Philippines campaign, commanded by Lieutenant General Hideyoshi Obata. The division, based in Formosa, had 4th Army Air Force Brigade at its disposal composed of four *sentais* (groups). The brigade had a mixed group of aircraft types from Kawasaki Ki-48 light bombers to Mitsubishi Ki-21 medium bombers. The IJAAF also had a number of Nakajima Ki-27 Nate fixed landing gear fighters. Although the primary Army fighter, at the time, it had limited success early in the war against obsolete Allied aircraft. The IJAAF recognized that this fighter could not match modern aircraft and it was withdrawn to Japan to serve as air defense interceptors and trainers. Obata could also use the 10th Independent Hikotai. This unit contained Mitsubishi Ki-15 reconnaissance, Mitsubishi Ki-36 air cooperation, and transport aircraft. The IJAAF aircraft had limited range, especially the Ki-27 fighters which could not operate over central Luzon from Formosa.

The IJN dedicated the 3rd Fleet under Vice-Admiral Ibo Takahashi, to support the IJA's invasion of the Philippines. The fleet, headquartered in the

In this posed photograph, Japanese soldiers show the typical armament used in the campaign. Armed with bolt-action Arisaka rifles, these soldiers would face a long and difficult fight for Bataan. (Tom Laemlein/Armor Plate Press)

Palau Islands, was to take the Philippines and later Borneo and the Celebes. Takahashi's role in the Philippines was to destroy the American naval forces, cover and support the IJA landings, and, with the invasions completed, protect IJA supply lines and reinforcements. The IJN did not have any large aircraft carriers available to support the Philippines operations, though Takahashi did have the light carrier *Ryujo* to conduct operations beyond the range of Japanese land-based aircraft. The fleet was composed largely of surface combatants that consisted of five heavy cruisers, five light cruisers, 29 destroyers, and two seaplane tenders. They also had some torpedo boats and minesweepers. The 3rd Fleet created surprise attack forces designated for the campaign to make the initial landings. The First (Aparri), Second (Vigan), Third (Batan Island), and Fourth (Legaspi) Surprise Attack Forces consisted of transports and an escort force of destroyers, minesweepers, and cruisers. Since the Asiatic Fleet offered little opposition, the IJN did not require much of a surface fleet to handle the American Navy. The 2nd Fleet also temporarily transferred several cruisers and destroyers to help Takahashi's force to provide fire support and to counter any American attempts, air or naval, to sink the invasion fleet. These were called the Northern and Southern Philippine Covering Forces.

The IJNAF provided a valued service to Homma early in the campaign. IGHQ planners assigned the 11th Air Fleet to the campaign consisting of the 21st and 23rd Air Flotillas based in Formosa, like the 5th Army Air Force Division. The 21st Air Flotilla provided Mitsubishi G4M1 (Betty) and G3M2 (Nell) twin-engine long-range bombers. The IJNAF's major contribution to the Philippines operation was the 23rd Air Flotilla that consisted of its fighter forces. Their naval fighters had a longer range than the IJAAF ones. IJNAF pilots did fly Mitsubishi A5M4 fixed landing gear fighters, but its most important contribution was the longer-range, Mitsubishi A6M2 Zero fighter. The Zero outclassed any FEAF fighter based in the Philippines. The IJNAF had 108 Zero fighters as part of its 304-strong force. These naval aircraft could reach targets in central Luzon, including the main FEAF base at Clark Field and Manila.

ORDERS OF BATTLE

US AND PHILIPPINE ORDER OF BATTLE

USAFFE

North Luzon Force
- PA 11th Division
- PA 21st Division
- PA 31st Division
- 26th Cavalry Regiment (PS)

South Luzon Force
- PA 1st Regular Division
- PA 41st Division
- PA 51st Division
- PA 71st Division

Visayan-Mindanao Force
- PA 61st Division
- PA 81st Division
- PA 101st Division

Manila and Subic Bay Harbor Defenses

Other forces
- Philippine Division
  - 31st Infantry Regiment
  - 45th Infantry Regiment (PS)
  - 57th Infantry Regiment (PS)
  - Division Artillery
- 1st Provisional Tank Group
  - 192nd Tank Battalion
  - 194th Tank Battalion
- 86th Field Artillery Battalion (PS, 155mm)
- 88th Field Artillery Regiment (PS, 75mm)
- 200th Coastal Artillery Regiment

US ASIATIC FLEET

USS *Houston* (CA-30 flagship)
USS *Marblehead* (CL-12)
USS *Boise* (CL-47)

Destroyer Squadron 29
- USS *Black Hawk* (AD-9)
- USS *Paul Jones* (DD230, flagship)

Destroyer Division 57
- USS *Whipple* (DD-217, flagship)
- USS *Alden* (DD-211)
- USS *John D. Edwards* (DD-216)
- USS *Edsall* (DD-219)

Destroyer Division 58
- USS *Stewart* (DD-224, flagship)
- USS *Parrott* (DD-218)
- USS *Barker* (DD-213)
- USS *Bulmer* (DD-222)

Destroyer Division 59
- USS *John D. Ford* (DD-228, flagship)
- USS *Pope* (DD-225)
- USS *Peary* (DD-226)
- USS *Pillsbury* (DD-227)

Submarine Squadron 29
- USS *Holland* (AS-3)
- USS *Canopus* (AS-9)
- USS *Otus* (AS-20)
- USS *Pigeon* (ASR-6)

Submarine Division 21
- USS *Salmon* (SS-182)
- USS *Seal* (SS-183)
- USS *Skipjack* (SS-184)
- USS *Sargo* (SS-188)
- USS *Saury* (SS-189)
- USS *Spearfish* (SS-190)

Submarine Division 22
- USS *Snapper* (SS-185)

USS *Stingray* (SS-186)
USS *Sturgeon* (SS-187)
USS *Sculpin* (SS-191)
USS *Sailfish* (SS-192)
USS *Swordfish* (SS-193)

Submarine Division 201
- USS *S-36* (SS-141)
- USS *S-37* (SS-142)
- USS *S-38* (SS-143)
- USS *S-39* (SS-144)
- USS *S-40* (SS-145)
- USS *S-41* (SS-146)

Submarine Division 202
- USS *Seadragon* (SS-194)
- USS *Sealion* (SS-195)
- USS *Searaven* (SS-196)
- USS *Seawolf* (SS-197)

Submarine Division 203
- USS *Porpoise* (SS-172)
- USS *Pike* (SS-173)
- USS *Shark* (SS-174)
- USS *Tarpon* (SS-175)
- USS *Perch* ((SS-176)
- USS *Pickeral* (SS-177)
- USS *Permit* (SS-178)

Patrol Wing Ten
- USS *Langley* (AV-3)
- USS *Childs* (AVD-1)
- USS *William R. Preston* (AVD-7)
- USS *Heron* (AVP-2)

Patrol Squadron 101 (VP-101)
- 18 PBY-4s

Patrol Squadron 102 (VP-102)
- 18 PBY-4s

Utility Squadron 10
- 1 JSF-2
- 3 JSF-4s
- 5 OS2U-2s
- 1 SOC-1

Other Asiatic Fleet Units

Mine Squadron 3
- Mine Division 8
- Mine Division 9

Motor Torpedo Boast Squadron 3

FAR EAST AIR FORCE

V Interceptor Command, Clark Field
- 24th Pursuit Group
  - 3rd Pursuit Squadron, Iba Field, 18 P-40Es
  - 17th Pursuit Squadron, Nichols Field, 18 P-40Es
  - 20th Pursuit Squadron, Clark Field, 18 P-40Bs
- 35th Pursuit Group (attached to the 24th Pursuit Group, headquarters not established)
  - 21st Pursuit Squadron, Nichols Field, 18 P-40Es
  - 34th Pursuit Squadron, Del Carmen Field, 18 P-35As

V Bomber Command Clark Field
- 19th Bombardment Group, Clark Field, 3 B-17s
  - 28th Bomb Squadron, Clark Field, 8 B-17s
  - 30th Bomb Squadron, Clark Field, 8 B-17s
  - 14th Bomb Squadron, Del Monte, 8 B-17Ds
  - 93rd Bomb Squadron, Del Monte, 8 B-17Ds
- 2nd Observation Squadron, Nichols Field

Philippine Army Air Corps

JAPANESE ORDER OF BATTLE

IJA INVASION FORCES

14th Army
16th Division
    9th Infantry Regiment
    20th Infantry Regiment
    33rd Infantry Regiment
    22nd Mountain Artillery

48th Division
    1st Formosa Infantry Regiment
    2nd Formosa Infantry Regiment
    47th Infantry Regiment
    48th Mountain Artillery

65th Independent Mixed Brigade
    122nd Infantry Regiment
    141st Infantry Regiment
    142nd Infantry Regiment

4th Tank Regiment
7th Tank Regiment

IJN INVASION FORCES

Covering Force
    Northern Philippine Covering Force
        Heavy cruisers *Haguro, Maya*
        Light cruiser *Kuma*
        2 minesweepers
    Southern Philippine Covering Force
        Light carrier *Ryujo*
        Heavy cruisers *Haguro, Myoko Nachi* (flagship)
        Light cruiser *Jintsu*
        Destroyers *Shiokaze, Amatsukaze, Hayashiro, Kuroshio, Hatsukaze, Natsushio, Oyashiro*

First Surprise Attack Force (Aparri)
    Light cruiser *Natori* (Flagship)
    Destroyers *Fumizuki, Nagatuski, Satsuki, Minazuki, Harukaze, Hatakaze*
    3 minesweepers
    9 antisubmarine craft
    6 *Maru* transports

Second Surprise Attack Force (Vigan)
    Light cruiser *Naka* (flagship)
    Destroyers *Murasame, Yudachi, Harusame, Samidare, Asagumo, Minegumo, Natsugumo*
    6 minesweepers
    9 antisubmarine craft
    6 Maru transports

Third Surprise Attack Force (Batan Island)
    Destroyer *Yamagumo*
    2 Maru transports

Fourth Surprise Attack Force (Legaspi)
    Light cruiser *Nagara* (flagship)
    Destroyers *Yamakaze, Suzukaze, Kawakaze, Umikaze, Yukikaze, Tokitsukaze*
    Seaplane tenders *Chitose, Mizuho*
    2 minesweepers
    2 patrol boats
    Seven Maru transports
The Southern Philippine Covering Force was also assigned to this force.

IJNAF COMMITTED TO THE PHILIPPINES

11th Air Fleet, Takao, Formosa

21st Naval Air Flotilla, Tainan, Formosa
    1st Naval Air Group, Tainan, Formosa
        48 G3M2s
    Toko Naval Air Group, Palau Islands with operating locations on Formosa
        24 H6K4s
        2 H6K2s
        13 A5M4s
    Kanoya Naval Air Group, Taichu, Formosa
        36 G4M1s
    1001 Naval Air Group, Chiai, Formosa
        25 L3Y1s
        1 G6M
    21st Naval Air Flotilla Transport Unit, Tainan, Formosa

23rd Naval Air Flotilla, Takao, Formosa
    3rd Naval Air Group, Takao, Formosa
        53 A6M2s
        7 A5M4s
        9 C5M2s
    Tainan Naval Air Group, Tainan, Formosa
        54 A6M2s
        6 A5M4s
        8 C5M2s
    Takao Naval Air Group, Takao, Formosa
        72 G4M1s
    23rd Naval Air Flotilla Transport Unit, Takao, Formosa

IJAAF COMMITTED TO THE PHILIPPINES

14th Army
(air unit directly under control of 14th Army)
    24th Sentai, Chaochou/Pingtung Formosa 36 Ki-27s

5th Army Air Force Division, Heito, Formosa
4th Army Air Force Brigade
        8th Sentai, Chiatung, Formosa
        27 Ki-48s
        9 Ki-15s
        2 Ki-46s
        14th Sentai, Chauchou, Formosa
        18 Ki-21s
        16th Sentai, Chiatung, Formosa
        31 Ki-30s
        50th Sentai, Hengchun, Formosa
        36 Ki-27s

10th Independent Air Unit, Pingtung, Formosa
    13 Ki-51s
    10 Ki-36s
    1 Ki-9

OPPOSING PLANS

The Japanese developed their pre-war strategy to conquer the Philippines as part of the larger effort to maintain their empire. The national strategy sought to gain access to raw materials, which required the IJA and IJN to knock out the American and British military quickly. This entailed a well-coordinated and timed effort over vast distances throughout the Pacific. In contrast, American pre-war strategy was to execute a holding action against any Japanese attack, and then mount a counterattack when sufficient resources became available. However, MacArthur altered the approved strategy for the Philippines, one accepted by both the Army and Navy for years, to a more active defense of the islands. If MacArthur could fight the Japanese on the beaches, he might defeat them before they established themselves in the islands. Unfortunately, MacArthur and Hart differed on the appropriate American strategy for the Philippines. This schism would hinder the early defensive effort; though even if these leaders had agreed on a common approach, it would probably not have stopped the eventual Japanese victory.

JAPAN'S MOVE TO WAR

Tokyo faced a difficult decision by early 1941. The IGHQ contemplated the possibility of curtailing military operations in China and Manchuria without access to raw materials. Either the Japanese government had to back down and accommodate the American and British governments' concerns by withdrawing from French Indochina, or it would need to expand the conflict by going to war to get access to resources. If Tokyo submitted to Washington and London, then it risked losing its gains in China, Manchuria, and Southeast Asia. This move would seriously affect Japan's stance in Asia. Imperial leaders would lose "face" and be humiliated throughout the Pacific. This would adversely affect Tokyo's ability to create its Greater East Asia Co-Prosperity Sphere from states within the region to "free" them of Western colonialism and control. Without raw materials and other resources, Japan was subject to the whims of the Western powers. The Japanese image of itself as the dominant power in Asia would be shattered by this strategic retreat.

Negotiations with Washington were going nowhere. Tokyo would not retreat from Southeast Asia or China. Similarly, Washington would not end its embargoes. War seemed imminent. Not all in Tokyo had believed war should be waged against the Americans and British. Within the Japanese IGHQ, there had been two competing approaches advocated for Japanese

top-level strategy in Asia and the Pacific. The IJN had viewed its main threat coming from the war with the United States and Great Britain, with the US Pacific Fleet offering the strongest potential opposition to future Japanese expansion south and east. The US Navy could isolate Japan and blockade it. However, IJA senior officers had a more continental approach with most of its soldiers based in China, and for them the principal opponent was the Soviet Union. The April 1941 non-aggression pact removed this immediate threat, and by June 1941 the Soviets were at war with Germany. Initial German success in Operation *Barbarossa* made it appear that the Soviets might collapse leaving Moscow too busy to threaten Japanese interests in Manchuria and Korea. If German military forces defeated the Soviets, then the IJA could sweep into Russian-held territories. Still, the empire needed oil, steel, and rubber to fuel its war machine. A continental strategy would not help Tokyo move into Southeast Asia; it could in fact make the shortage of raw materials worse.

The Japanese government continued to negotiate with Washington throughout the summer and fall of 1941 with little success. By November 1941, the government decided it needed to strike into British-held Malaya and the Dutch territories in Borneo, Sumatra, Java, and the Celebes. Tokyo could wage a systematic war, attacking each of these targets in turn. However, this would give the Americans, British, and Dutch the opportunity of concentrating their forces and dragging the Japanese into a costly war of attrition. The other approach was to conduct a fast, multi-pronged offensive designed to overwhelm multiple opponents at the same time. The IGHQ would need to conduct a simultaneous air, land, and sea attack. The IJN would attempt to disable the Pacific Fleet at Pearl Harbor, which would eliminate the threat to the Japanese moves south and thwart any efforts to resupply American forces in the Philippines. The elimination of both the American Pacific Fleet and Royal Navy forces in the region would also ensure the safe passage of any raw materials from Southeast Asian conquests back to Japan. Meanwhile, IJN and IJA forces would conduct attacks against the Philippines and Malaya, especially Singapore, to neutralize any opposition to a further southern advance into the Netherlands East Indies. Taking the Philippines would also remove a potential American staging base for future operations by Washington to strike at the Japanese. The Japanese would also hit Hong Kong, Guam, Wake Island, and other targets. Although a risky campaign, Japanese surprise and military superiority could allow swift victories throughout the Pacific. The Americans would have no major bases near Japan to conduct a counterstrike. London was more concerned about German actions in Europe and North Africa, and the British might offer token responses only to avoid loss of its other major colony, India.

The plan for the Japanese attack into the Philippines included a combination of air attacks, amphibious landings, and occupation to conquer the islands. American forces in the Philippines presented a major threat to any advance south by Tokyo. Washington would probably oppose future Japanese military moves. Once the Japanese took the Philippines, the IJA and IJN could then focus on expanding into Malaya and the Netherlands East Indies. The IGHQ believed it would have to move swiftly to beat the Americans, British, and Dutch. If the Japanese could destroy American bases and forces in the Philippines and Hawaii quickly, then it could remove the one immediate major threat to Japan, the US Pacific Fleet. Japanese forces could then focus on the British and Dutch.

The Japanese plan involved their air forces first neutralizing the FEAF in the Philippines. Pre-war reconnaissance missions had located the FEAF bases and strengths for attack and IJAAF aircraft had responsibility for targets above 16 degrees north latitude and the IJNAF south of that point into central Luzon. Japanese control of the air was a prerequisite for a successful amphibious assault. The FEAF had B-17 strategic bombers that could hit Formosan targets, attack enemy naval forces, invasion fleets, or Japanese ground units. However, the Japanese knew that the FEAF also possessed many fighters that would oppose their efforts to control the air. Japanese planners hoped that simultaneous attacks on FEAF airfields might catch the American aircraft on the ground. Clark Field was the major US base with B-17s and P-40s and it was a priority target for the Japanese.

While IJNAF aircraft had the range to hit many targets in the Philippines, the critical problem facing the IJAAF's 5th Air Group was the short range of

Japanese amphibious operations at Lamon Bay and along the Lingayen Gulf used landing craft like these. These craft could carry about 80 personnel or two small tanks. They were shallow drafted vessels that had difficulty operating in poor weather conditions. (Tom Laemlein/ Armor Plate Press)

its fighters. Japanese plans prioritized seizure of airfields to extend the range of its fighters. A Japanese landing force was tasked with capturing Batan Island, about 100 miles north of Luzon. Its seizure would allow the IJAAF to extend the range of its fighters further over Luzon. The IJN would also conduct landings at Aparri, Vigan, and Legaspi in order extend the IJAAF bases and aircraft capabilities. Once the IJAAF and IJNAF attained air superiority, IJA units would then conduct major amphibious operations in Luzon and Mindanao.

Once the Japanese had swept the skies of enemy aircraft, it could concentrate on the US and Filipino ground forces. Homma's focus was on central Luzon which had the greatest concentrations of American military forces and Manila, the capital. IJA ground units were to land in the Lingayen Gulf and Lamon Bay areas in Luzon to act as pincers to surround and overcome the combined American-Filipino forces based there. Once the Japanese had overcome enemy resistance, the IJA could occupy Manila and other vital strategic locations. As Tokyo advanced on Manila, the IGHQ assumed it would defeat an American-Filipino force trying to defend the capital in a decisive battle. Manila would force, in Japanese eyes, an American and Philippine capitulation since it was the capital. After defeating the Americans, the IGHQ would redeploy part of Homma's IJA air and ground units to Malaya and the Netherlands East Indies. The Japanese, from the Palau Islands, also planned to seize areas in southern Mindanao as a jumping-off-point to initiate attacks on Jolo Island and then to Borneo. The IJN would also blockade the Philippines and isolate it from any reinforcements or resupply efforts.

The image of a defeated American Army would demonstrate to the world that Tokyo had supremacy in the Pacific. Homma had 50 days to end his campaign and he thought that his forces could win in 45 days. In the long term, Japan planned to conduct a limited war and defend its new territory before American industrial power could fully mobilize. Tokyo hoped to negotiate a peace settlement with the Americans and British. If that failed, the Japanese could create a defensive network of Pacific islands to wage a war of attrition.

AMERICAN DEFENSE OF THE PHILIPPINES

Washington had many concerns about the defense of the Philippines. If it was to grant the Commonwealth's freedom in 1946, then why should America devote a massive amount of resources to defend it, particularly with the effects

of the Great Depression still being felt at home? Many Army officers believed that the islands were indefensible given their vast and varied geography, current basing, and available forces. Naval leaders had consistently valued the Philippines as a naval base for future operations in the Far East, especially Subic Bay, but even they had growing doubts about its defense. The Joint Army and Navy Board's Planning Committee had developed a defense plan for the islands codenamed War Plan Orange (WPO), which was one of several developed before World War I and modified periodically to reflect any change in national policy or perceived threat. Differences of opinion between the various services constantly surfaced throughout the process.

American military forces in the Philippines

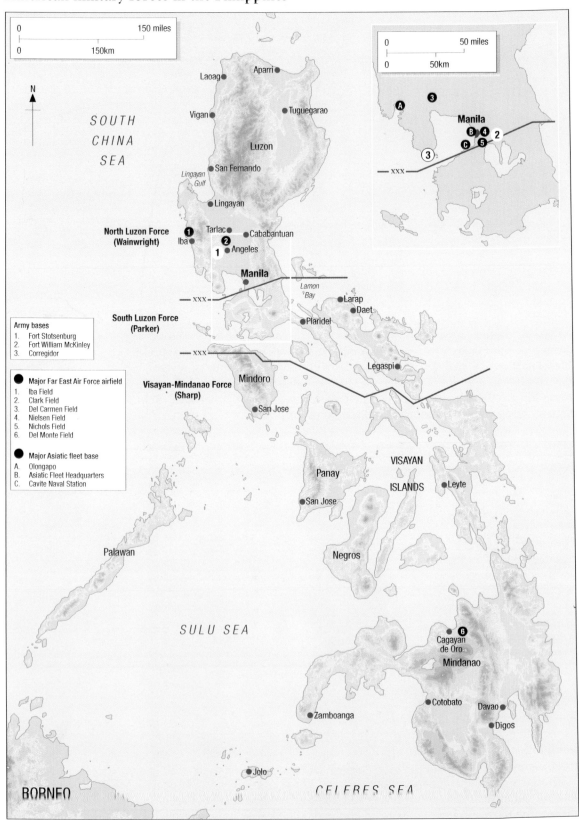

Army bases
1. Fort Stotsenburg
2. Fort William McKinley
3. Corregidor

● Major Far East Air Force airfield
1. Iba Field
2. Clark Field
3. Del Carmen Field
4. Nielsen Field
5. Nichols Field
6. Del Monte Field

● Major Asiatic fleet base
A. Olongapo
B. Asiatic Fleet Headquarters
C. Cavite Naval Station

North Luzon Force
(Wainwright)

South Luzon Force
(Parker)

Visayan-Mindanao Force
(Sharp)

SOUTH CHINA SEA

Laoag
Aparri
Vigan
Tuguegarao
Luzon
San Fernando
Lingayan Gulf
Lingayan
Tarlac
Cababantuan
Iba
Angeles
Manila
Lamon Bay
Larap
Daet
Plaridel
Legaspi
Mindoro
San Jose
VISAYAN ISLANDS
Leyte
Panay
San Jose
Negros
Palawan
SULU SEA
Cagayan de Oro
Mindanao
Cotobato
Davao
Zamboanga
Digos
Jolo
BORNEO
CELEBES SEA

Manila

LEFT
Japanese forces had a huge advantage over the Americans with regards to their supply and logistic situation. Homma could get supplies from Formosa or direct from Japan. MacArthur placed his hopes on reinforcements from the American West Coast. Here, Japanese soldiers unload supplies to feed its military machine. (US Army)

RIGHT
MacArthur's plans included efforts to try to entangle the Japanese on the beach. If he could hold and defeat an invader at the beach, then he might retain control of the Philippines. (US Army)

WPO-3 was the last revision before the Japanese attacked, approved in April 1941. It envisioned Americans and Filipinos defending the islands with little warning. Washington incorporated WPO-3 into the Rainbow-5 set of war plans that prioritized an active war against Germany rather than Japan. Any defense of the Philippines would have to be based on existing forces with no prospect of immediate reinforcement. Naval officers on the Joint Board believed the Japanese could land up to 60,000 men on the Philippines within a week, with another 100,000 a week later. Total Japanese forces could then amount to around 300,000 within a month. The Japanese would then overwhelm limited American and Filipino units. With the limited American presence available, Navy planners believed it would not be possible stop the Japanese.

Under WPO-3, after limited resistance on Luzon, the American and Filipino forces were to retreat into the Bataan Peninsula, the objective of the plan being to defend Manila Bay and deny its control to the Japanese. Without Manila Bay, the capture of capital and Luzon would be incomplete. Harbor defenses, based on fortified islands in Manila Bay and Bataan, would protect the bay's entrance. The Pacific Fleet would then fight its way through to the Philippines and reinforce the defenders within six months. Presumably, by this stage the Navy would have bested the IJN's Combined Fleet. American planners hoped its forces could hold out against a massive attack and wait for the Pacific Fleet to deliver reinforcements which would then push the Japanese out.

MacArthur believed WPO-3 was "defeatist." He insisted on planning a more active defense. MacArthur wanted to defend any invasion at the point of landing, not retreat to Bataan immediately. The plan was to attack the enemy while they were on the beaches, when they were vulnerable. He thought the best chance of defeating a Japanese invasion was to prevent the enemy from establishing a foothold on Luzon. MacArthur's enthusiasm for the value of untested PA reserve divisions, his long-range B-17s and growing fighter force, and the planned and shipped reinforcements from the United States bolstered Washington's confidence in his position. AAF officers also thought a sufficient B-17 force might deter a Japanese invasion since they believed that they could destroy an invasion fleet or hit Japanese bases in Formosa. If the Americans had enough time to reinforce the Philippines, train the burgeoning PA, and build defenses then they had a chance to halt a Japanese offense. Marshall agreed and thought MacArthur might hold out, at least for a time. Additional military aid and personnel streamed into the Philippines. MacArthur assumed that any invasion would not take place until April 1942 due to weather conditions. The fall and winter brought unsuitable weather for any amphibious landing operations. Given this extra time, MacArthur's forces would have constructed proper beach defenses, trained the PA divisions, and prepared the FEAF to defend the islands.

Hart took a different view on the defense of the Philippines. His relatively small Asiatic Fleet stood little chance against the IJN and Hart proposed, on September 17, 1941, to deploy most of his surface fleet south of the Philippines and combine it with the Royal Navy. This combined fleet would then be a better counter to the IJN. By October 27, Hart had significantly modified his position following discussions with MacArthur; he proposed that his surface fleet operate out of Manila Bay supporting the Army plan. The Chief of Naval Operations, Admiral Harold Stark, disapproved and many other naval officers still believed that the defense of the Philippines was a lost cause. Sending in any reinforcements was a tremendous waste and fighting the Japanese piecemeal was suicidal. Hart prepared his surface fleet to retreat south to fight with the combined Royal Navy and Dutch ships. Asiatic Fleet submarines and PT boats would attack any invasion force, but they too would move south when they lost their support bases.

Without naval cability to counter an invasion fleet or to protect any resupply convoys, the Philippines seemed doomed. Conversely, the Asiatic Fleet had little chance of successfully opposing the IJN's ships, and future naval capabilities were at risk if the IJN destroyed the Asiatic Fleet. The American forces in the Philippines faced the Japanese with a divided strategy, and the only victor in such a situation was Tokyo.

THE BATTLE FOR THE PHILIPPINES

While IJN forces attacked Pearl Harbor and other Hawaiian bases on the morning of December 7, 1941, American leaders in the Philippines were asleep. Asiatic Fleet Headquarters radio communications personnel received a message from the Commander-in-Chief, Pacific, Admiral Husband Kimmel that the Japanese had bombed Pearl Harbor. The local time was 0230hrs on December 8 in Manila. An aide woke Hart, but no one notified MacArthur or any Army officer. Army Signal Corps operators intercepted a commercial radio transmission that confirmed the news about the surprise attack on Hawaii about a half hour later. Due to the time-zone difference, the Japanese would have to wait a few hours to begin their operations against the Philippines and other targets in their southward advance, since it was still too dark to conduct aircraft operations. This was a major risk to the IGHQ. With the early attack on Pearl Harbor, Japanese leaders believed that they would fight alerted Americans in prepared defenses.

MacArthur and Hart seemed to have ample warning time to notify their subordinates and get ready for the anticipated Japanese attack. American Army units had time to start notifying PA reserve divisions and moving units to defensive positions along the Luzon coastal areas. Hart could have ordered Asiatic Fleet surface ship commanders to steam south, and warned submariners patrolling Luzon to watch for any possible invasion fleets. Brereton had the opportunity to direct FEAF bomber squadron commanders to move or protect their aircraft. He also could have sent up fighter patrols. MacArthur's active defense plan was now going to face its biggest test. MacArthur was confident that he could protect the islands when he told Hart "I am going to fight a glorious land war." He believed that if Japanese invaded the Philippines his combined American and Filipino forces would "crush them."

JAPANESE AIR SUPERIORITY AND THE BUMBLING NINCOMPOOPS

The IGHQ's immediate campaign task was to gain air superiority. A vital objective was the destruction of the FEAF's interceptor and bomber commands, the largest US air force outside the continental United States. Japanese air forces would hit FEAF bases and forces. The key targets were the fighter bases at Iba, Nichols Field, Del Carmen, and Clark Field. The Japanese knew the Americans had concentrated their FEAF forces at these bases and the only one of these installations that the IJNAF could not hit was Del Monte

in Mindanao. The Japanese considered the B-17 bases at Clark and Del Monte Fields a threat, but the most important goal was to knock out the FEAF P-40s. Without the P-40s, the IJAAF and IJNAF could attack the Americans and Filipinos at will.

Japanese air-reconnaissance aircraft had conducted missions over the Philippines as late as December 5. These missions had provided a visible warning to MacArthur's staff of potential combat and MacArthur had even given the order to attack any Japanese aircraft conducting further reconnaissance flights. Bases went on alert and FEAF officers had prepared aircraft dispersal orders. Japanese air commanders possessed knowledge of American force disposition before hostilities and prepared their targets. Other forces did not provide as lucrative targets to the IJAAF and IJNAF. The Asiatic Fleet offered few substantial aircraft targets. The Navy did not have any fighters, only a patrol wing of PBY-4 Catalina search planes and a few observation aircraft. The burgeoning PA Air Corps had obsolete P-26A Peashooter fighters that did not offer much resistance.

FEAF commanders worked hard to prepare for an air assault. MacArthur had received SCR-270, 272, and 371 air radar-warning units, but only one set was operational at Iba. By 1942, the Americans would have three warning detector locations and one information center operational, with the only personnel trained to operate the radars coming from a single company of 200 personnel. The ground air defenses also included the American 60th and 200th Coastal Artillery Regiments, but they did not have enough weapons to protect the airfields, the fortified islands at Manila Bay's mouth, Subic Bay, Manila, and other bases. Antiaircraft defenses consisted of only 24 machine guns at Clark Field and Manila. The major effort to protect FEAF aircraft would have to come from combat air patrols combined with the dispersal of aircraft to secondary airfields.

Brereton initiated planning for a retaliatory B-17 bombing strike against Formosa slated for the morning of December 8. At 0500hrs Brereton attempted to get MacArthur's approval for the bombing mission, but his request had to go through MacArthur's chief of staff Brigadier General

Richard K. Sutherland. Sutherland was a difficult man to work through since he was so protective of MacArthur. Sutherland insisted that MacArthur was too busy and that Brereton should prepare his bombers for the mission, but Sutherland would release approval to him only once MacArthur concurred. The FEAF would also need current intelligence on Japanese forces on Formosa anyway and that would require a new photographic reconnaissance mission since the pre-war information on Formosa might be inaccurate. Events surrounding the approval of the bombing mission remain shrouded in controversy to this day.

Brereton checked with Sutherland to see if MacArthur had approved the mission at 0700hrs, while the FEAF still required new reconnaissance data to update target folders. The reconnaissance pilots faced problems with cloudy conditions over Formosa. A B-17 had taken off at 0800hrs to conduct a photographic mission over Formosa, but it turned back due to mechanical problems. Brereton believed that at least poor weather conditions would mean that the Japanese would be unable to undertake operations as well. He ordered the remaining 16 B-17s based at Del Monte to move by night to an auxiliary field at San Marcelino to prepare to bomb Formosa the next morning.

IJNAF aircraft would spearhead any airstrike against major FEAF bases in central Luzon and, since most of the IJN carriers had deployed to Hawaii, the only option was to use ground-based aircraft. These forces were to fly from Formosa to Clark, about 500 miles away. IJN Combined Fleet officers also allocated the light carrier *Ryujo* for the assault against Davao in southern Mindanao since it was out of range of IJNAF aircraft from Formosa. The US Navy maintained a naval base at Davao which could prove a danger to both the IJN's base in the Palau Islands about 500 miles east and a proposed landing in southern Luzon at Legaspi. However, none of the Navy aircraft appeared able to contest the IJNAF or IJN surface ships.

While the FEAF awaited orders, the weather had cleared over Formosa and Japanese aircraft started flying towards the Philippines bases. IJAAF and IJNAF pilots took off around Formosa at 0700hrs and reports of Japanese bomber aircraft flying south reached Brereton at 0900hrs, probably from the radar at Iba. At 0930hrs, Japanese aircraft struck Tuguegarao with 25 Kawasaki Ki-48 Lily bombers. Another IJNAF force of 17 Mitsubishi Ki-21s hit Baguio, the summer capital of the Philippines where Quezon was staying, though he was unhurt. Reports filtered through to Manila and MacArthur's forces now knew they were under Japanese aerial assault.

Brereton had pushed his FEAF crews and aircraft to prepare for a morning attack by the Japanese and the remaining FEAF B-17s at Clark scrambled into the air when reports of the attacks on Baguio and Tuguegarao came through; some pilots flew without full fuel tanks and none were loaded with bombs. Clark put up its 15 flyable B-17s into the air to avoid a repeat of the Japanese catching aircraft on the ground as had happened at Hawaii. Fighters also took to the skies to provide combat air patrols over the airfields.

The IJAAF attacks also pushed Brereton into contacting Sutherland again at 1000hrs about the B-17 bombing missions over Formosa. Brereton recalled that he received a call from MacArthur at 1014hrs and mentioned to him that he would have to delay any bombing mission till the afternoon due to a lack of current reconnaissance information. Meanwhile, B-17s had searched areas north of Luzon looking for enemy aircraft or any sign of an invasion. After the attacks on Baguio and Tuguegarao, observers reported that the IJAAF bombers had headed home to Formosa. The FEAF had issued an all-

ATTACK ON CLARK FIELD, DECEMBER 8, 1941 (pp. 36–37)

In a massive air attack just after noon on December 8, 1941, IJNAF G3M Nell and G4M1 Betty bombers, plus escorting A6M2 Zero fighter escorts, struck the FEAF base at Clark Field on Luzon. Japanese commanders and planners had long realized the importance of airpower for their operational success and Homma needed to establish complete Japanese air superiority to ensure the success of his invasion. His first task, therefore, was to destroy the FEAF. The IJNAF was tasked with neutralizing the AAF fighters and bombers in central Luzon and a critical factor was the range of its main fighter, the Zero. The Zeros could reach Clark, unlike the short-range IJAAF fighters. These considerations led to the IJNAF leading missions against Iba, Clark, and other targets around Manila. Despite ample warnings provided by the attack on Pearl Harbor, the Japanese were able to attack the AAF bases without major opposition. At Clark, the

Japanese bombers first attacked hangars and parked Boeing B-17C/D bombers and P-40B/E fighters. Clark-based fighters had taken to the air to protect the base, but at the time of the Japanese strike many of the P-40s needed to land to refuel. In this scene, the IJNAF Betty bombers have completed their bombing runs over Clark and Zeros from the 23rd Air Flotilla, Tainan Naval Air Group, strafe the remaining parked B-17 and P-40s **(1)**. Four P-40B fighters from the 20th Pursuit Squadron managed to get airborne during the attack and engaged the Japanese aircraft **(2)**. These AAF fighters could deliver heavy firepower with six .30-cal. machine guns. The P-40Bs managed to shoot down several Zeros **(3)**, but could not stop Clark's destruction. A Zero piloted by IJNAF ace Saburo Sakai is shown at the right-hand side of the drawing **(4)**. Sakai was Japan's greatest ace in the war.

clear report at around 1000hrs. The air attacks seemed over and the B-17s and fighters returned to their bases. By 1100, the B-17s and fighters started landing, with the fighters needing to refuel. General Brereton finally received approval to mount his raid on Formosa at 1120hrs. Some Clark-based P-40s started to land at 1230hrs. Aircraft from Iba and Nichols Field also had to return. Other pursuit squadrons, at Nichols and Del Carmen, stood ready to scramble and cover Clark and the other fighter installations.

Land-based IJNAF bombers and A6M2 Zeros had left their Formosan bases to hit the major FEAF airfields further south than the IJAAF. An IJNAF force of 108 Mitsubishi G3M2 Nell and G4M1 Betty bombers, plus 84 Mitsubishi A6M2 Zero fighters, headed for Clark and Iba. FEAF commanders received some warning reports of aircraft heading south over the Lingayen Gulf at 1137hrs, and at 1145hrs FEAF Headquarters at Nielson Field sent immediate warnings to Clark. Radio and teletype messages did not reach the appropriate Clark officials and officers took no action.

IJNAF fighters struck Iba first at 1235hrs destroying a flight of P-40s while they attempted to land. Other Iba P-40s had to divert to Clark. With many of Iba's aircraft and early warning capabilities destroyed, the IJNAF aircraft flew on towards Clark to press the attack.

The main Japanese air attack force caught almost all of Clark's aircraft on the ground at 1240hrs. Few pursuit aircraft met the Japanese attackers. Pilots did attempt to get into the air, but the Zeros shot many of them down or damaged their planes. IJNAF bombers and fighters repeatedly attacked the field. IJNAF pilots also struck Del Carmen where FEAF crews flew Seversky P-35A fighters, who attempted to engage the Zeros, but were outclassed and overwhelmed.

In a single day, the IJNAAF and IJNAF repeated the successes of Pearl Harbor. Only 17 B-17s remained operational and the AAF fighter force suffered 53 P-40 and three P-35A losses. The Japanese also shot up 25 to 30 other aircraft including obsolete observation, training, B-10 and B-18 bombers, and transport aircraft. Only seven Zeros failed to return to Formosa. Half of the FEAF was shattered and these attacks meant that the Japanese would have air superiority for the rest of the campaign.

When MacArthur heard about the successful IJAAF and IJNAF strikes he was livid. The Japanese had annihilated his air forces; accusations flew to and fro about who was responsible. The Japanese aerial reconnaissance missions flown before December 8 should have forced MacArthur to keep his FEAF aircraft dispersed. Coupled with the many warnings from Washington, MacArthur had ordered all 35 B-17s moved from Clark to Del Monte Field in Mindanao on December 1. This action would have spared the B-17s from destruction since they would have been 500 miles south of Clark. Only half of the bombers left for their new base. Arnold, MacArthur, and Roosevelt were never fully satisfied with the reasons why the Japanese destroyed half of the bombers and many fighters on the ground. Denials and counterdenials were exchanged between Brereton, Sutherland, and MacArthur about the delays and requests for the bombing attacks on Formosa, moving the B-17s to Del Monte, and protecting the airfields.

The Philippine defense forces were now vulnerable to further Japanese air attacks while the remaining FEAF aircraft had to move south to avoid further destruction. With Japanese aircraft destroying the air-warning radar at Iba, only aircraft and ground observers could provide limited air warning. The loss of the FEAF also limited the number of B-17s available to search for the IJN, leaving only the PBYs and submarine patrols to spot any invasion convoys.

The Japanese invasion force was composed mostly of infantry units. Devoid of truck transportation, Japanese forces in Southeast Asia relied on bicycles like these troops in the Philippines. (US Army)

Japanese bombing missions continued with 13 IJNAF dive-bombers and nine fighters from the *Ryujo* bombing and strafing Davao in the early morning of December 8. The US Navy seaplane tender USS *William B. Pearson* escaped south, but IJNAF aircraft destroyed two PBYs and rendered the base useless.

One of MacArthur's main tools to stop the Japanese, his B-17s, now lay shattered at Clark. He would later claim that a B-17 assault on Formosa would have been a suicidal mission anyway. The B-17C/Ds in the Philippines contained fewer defensive weapons than later versions that flew over Europe. Additionally, his P-40s did not have the range to escort the B-17s to Formosa and return to Clark. IJAAF and IJNAF fighters might well have inflicted heavy casualties on the B-17s flying over Formosa. MacArthur put the blame on Brereton and his deputy commander whom he branded as "bumbling nincompoops."

The Japanese were ready to resume major air operations the following day, but weather grounded all aircraft on Formosa. The IJAAF and IJNAF still had several targets left, including the naval installations at Olongapo in Subic Bay and the Asiatic Fleet's shipyard at Cavite in Manila Bay.

By December 10, Homma ordered the landing of IJA forces on Aparri and Vigan as the IJAAF and IJNAF now had air superiority. IJA troops on IJN transports sailed from their Formosan harbors on December 7. Three IJA landing forces left the Palau Islands for targets in southern Luzon and Jolo Island, between Mindanao and Borneo. An earlier landing force had taken Batan Island unopposed on December 8. The IJA landed 490 soldiers and found a small airfield on the island that needed considerable improvement if it were to become useable.

The planned extension of IJAAF airfields proved unnecessary once the IJNAF had destroyed Clark and Iba. IJNAF officers still had to eliminate Del Carmen, Nichols, and Nielson and 54 IJNAF bombers struck Cavite destroying its power plant, supply building, and machine shops. Japanese aircraft also wrecked the submarine *Sealion*. Japanese reports following the Philippines campaign indicated that the most important target destroyed was the submarine torpedo supply. The bombers also hit Manila, while defenders at Nielson and some outlying fields saw 27 bombers and 36 fighters smash aircraft and facilities. Eighteen fighters struck Nichols. At Del Carmen, Zeros destroyed 12 and damaged six P-35s on the ground. The FEAF had few remaining fighters, about 30 P-40s along with a few obsolete P-35As and P-26s.

Once the hostilities had erupted, Hart ordered his major surface fleet south according to the Navy's plan. The destruction of the FEAF had convinced Hart that there was little that his fleet could do. Submarines, PT boats, and a few surface ships remained to hinder the Japanese amphibious forces. The rest of the Asiatic Fleet joined with the British and Dutch as a combined force in Borneo to oppose future Japanese moves.

THE JAPANESE INVASION OF LUZON

Despite the presence of American aircraft in Luzon, albeit a small number, Japanese leaders proceeded with its planned landings. Homma and the 14th Army were to conduct the initial ground operations on Luzon at Vigan and Aparri on December 10.

The first Japanese landing soldiers came from the 2nd Formosa Infantry Regiment, 48th Division. Each Japanese task force at the two sites was to include one and a half battalions and support units, roughly 2,000 men. The Aparri invasion force was the Tanaka Detachment while the Kanno Detachment headed the Vigan force.

The Aparri IJN First Surprise Attack Force started operations off the coast at dawn on December 10. Under poor weather conditions, the IJN landing craft had difficulty coming ashore in the rising surf. Only two companies landed unopposed at Aparri, the rest of the Tanaka Detachment came ashore 20 miles to the east. The IJA faced no opposition, even though MacArthur's staff had realized that if the Japanese took Aparri it would extend the IJAAF's range through the seizure of the airfield. The active defense plan failed to

A stylized Japanese rendition of an IJA action against the Americans demonstrates the ferocity of combat between the two foes. Despite a lack of supplies, equipment, and trained Filipino reserve forces, MacArthur's forces managed to disrupt the IJA schedule for the conquest of the Philippines. (US Army)

stop the IJA from hitting the beach and establishing a foothold. The next day, the 50th Sentai, composed of about 36 Ki-27s, was operational from Aparri. The only casualties of the operation were a wrecked minesweeper and a destroyer and a light cruiser damaged by American air attack.

Japan's Second Surprise Attack Force also prepared to disembark at Vigan. As the Kanno Detachment began to come ashore, a P-40 radioed a report of the invasion to the FEAF at 0513hrs. The FEAF then attacked with B-17s and P-40s thwarting the main invasion attempt, which was delayed by a day – though some Kanno Detachment units did land at Pandan and later seized Vigan. The American air attack managed to destroy one minesweeper and beach two transports. A B-17C, piloted by Captain Colin Kelly, allegedly bombed the IJN battleship *Haruna*, though this was later proved false. Washington made Kelly the first AAF hero of the war after he allowed his crew to bail out and died trying to land the plane.

The next day, the remaining Kanno Detachment units tried to land again. Weather had inhibited IJA units from going ashore and the fleet had to move four miles south to disembark the troops. After consolidating on the coast, Kanno Detachment elements headed to Laoag where IJA soldiers took the town and airfield.

Homma also wanted to take part of southeastern Luzon. From the Palau Islands the 16th Division, commanded by Major General Naoki Kimura, sent approximately 2,500 men to take Legaspi. The earlier *Ryujo* raid on Davao had eliminated any American naval air threat and IJNAF aircraft from the *Ryujo* could support the landings. An American submarine had witnessed the Fourth Special Attack Force steaming from the west on December 6. The invasion fleet met no resistance and the Kimura Detachment disembarked on December 12. Kimura's forces took the city with its airfield and a major railroad junction.

The air situation for MacArthur was precarious. With fewer fighters and the Japanese in Legaspi and attacks on Davao, the IJNAF would soon find its way to the remaining B-17s at Del Monte. Continual operations and flying at the newly constructed base at Del Monte put a strain on the maintenance crews, limited facilities, fuel, ordnance, and spare parts. With the main bomber base at Clark heavily damaged and the Japanese aircraft in range, Brereton requested permission to remove all B-17s from Del Monte to Batchelor Field near Darwin, Australia. The flyable B-17s escaped by December 17. Four Zeros based at Legaspi did attack Del Monte on December 19 and shot up three B-18s. B-17 pilots would now have to fly 1,500 miles from Australia to conduct future bombing sorties against Mindanao, and about 2,000 miles to Luzon. The Navy's remaining Patrol Wing of ten PBY-4s also left the Philippines for Borneo. The main FEAF support would now come from the remaining P-40s, but attrition, lack of spare parts, and aviation fuel crippled their availability.

THE JAPANESE STRIKE SOUTH

The IJA's 16th Army helped Homma to take Davao in southern Mindanao. Davao's airfield provided a base to expand further south, and the IGHQ could then take Jolo Island in the Sulu Sea to further attacks on Borneo. The Sakaguchi Detachment from the IJA's 56th Division's 146th Infantry Regiment came ashore at 0400hrs on 20 December, a total Japanese strength of about 5,000 soldiers. Elements of the PA's 101st Division held Davao, but some units withdrew soon after the Japanese landed on Luzon.

TO FILIPINOS IN DAVAO

The Japanese Forces have already landed. They have come to free you and all your brethren in the Philippines. Japan is not fighting the Philippines but only America so give the Americans no cooperation. They are your real enemies. We are your friends. Do not mistreat Japanese in Davao for they are your best friends. Japanese Forces will give Filipinos every consideration, but if you harm the local Japanese in any way, the punishment will be severe.

ANY HARM DONE TO JAPANESE RESIDENTS WILL BE DEALT WITH SEVERELY.

The Japanese landing at Davao faced little opposition. The city had a sizable Japanese population that provided valuable information to the landing force. This leaflet urges the Filipino population to accept Japanese control while warning them to do no harm to Japanese residents. (US Air Force)

By the afternoon, the IJA had taken Davao and Japanese airfield construction crews prepared a seaplane base and awaited the arrival of IJNAF aircraft. Bombing attacks by eight Kawanishi H6K flying boats targeted Del Monte. Zeros from Davao now had the range to strafe targets in southern Luzon and the Japanese forces slowly isolated the Philippines. Any convoys of replacements from Hawaii or the West Coast would have to run a gauntlet of IJN surface and air forces.

The Japanese did not require the entire Sakaguchi Detachment to control the captured city. The Miura Detachment stayed on at Davao while some of the Sakaguchi Detachment with Naval Special Landing Forces ventured to Jolo Island. This force landed on Christmas Eve and encountered scant resistance. Japanese forces were poised to advance west into the Netherlands East Indies and the IGHQ had a stepping-stone to enter Borneo.

DEFENDING NORTHERN LUZON

MacArthur now had to face a major Japanese invasion. Early in the campaign, MacArthur's staff had correctly identified the Aparri and Vigan landings as secondary attacks to acquire airfields; the Japanese main landings now awaited. Wainwright, responsible for defending northern Luzon, had several concerns. On paper, the PA had adequate numbers of troops, but they were still ill trained, poorly equipped, and lacked experienced officers. The vast area, lack of armored forces, inadequate artillery, no antitank weapons, and scant air support crippled Wainwright. With little hope for rapid reinforcement, MacArthur had to fight with what he had.

MacArthur had limited options. The FEAF had few remaining aircraft to fight and, after Pearl Harbor and the Philippines, Washington now had to organize a defense for Hawaii, Alaska, the Panama Canal, and the rest of the United States. The public was in fear of a Japanese invasion along the West Coast. Still, Roosevelt and Marshall had promised MacArthur aid. The AAF's Arnold wanted to send MacArthur B-24s through Cairo to expand the USAFFE's striking power. Calls for an additional 230 pursuit aircraft went to Washington. Some officers in the War and Navy Departments continued to argue that there was no point in sending more resources to a lost cause. MacArthur still believed that a convoy, headed by a carrier, could break through to him; however, the Pacific Fleet could not risk a loss of one. He also advocated that the Chinese should start a major offensive against the Japanese and that Washington should try to get the Soviets to attack IJA forces in Manchuria. Washington had another issue to deal with, the agreed-upon strategy of concentrating on Europe first and then Japan. The Americans and British confirmed this priority at the Arcadia Conference held in Washington starting on December 22 and concluding on January 14, 1942. The diversion of resources to MacArthur would run directly against this strategy.

Still, American and Filipino forces prepared for the imminent main IJA assault. The most likely invasion site was in the Lingayen Gulf, which had a direct route to Manila – the assumed IGHQ objective. IJA forces had already taken Legaspi, but could also take another southern site, at Lamon Bay on the east coast of Luzon, southeast of Manila. IJA landings at Vigan, Aparri, and Legaspi made MacArthur's strategy of attacking any invading Japanese forces at the beaches moot. MacArthur modified his directives to Wainwright to shorten his responsibility of defense from all of northern Luzon to the area south of San Fernando on the coast.

American and Filipino forces responded. Wainwright's North Luzon force sent the 11th Division and the PS 26th Cavalry to defend the Lingayen Gulf area near San Fernando. A regiment from the 71st Division moved from Mindanao, and Wainwright assigned it to stop the Kanno and Tanaka Detachments moving south to link up with any future invasion force. The area north of San Fernando was mountainous and the PA units were to hold the areas where coastal Route 3 and interior Route 5 passed through this difficult terrain. The Philippine Division served as the strategic reserve along with the tank reinforcements. Wainwright could still call on the 21st Division to hold the area near Lingayen and 31st Division north of Subic Bay.

Although Wainwright lacked organic tank and armored cars in his divisions and units, MacArthur did make available the two National Guard tank battalions of 108 M3 Stuart light tanks and M3 half-tracks with M1897 75mm guns. These obsolete ex-French 75mm field guns offered a counter to Japanese tanks and could deliver direct fire support. Although Wainwright could call on the tanks for support, MacArthur did not place them under his direct control. MacArthur could also call on the 4th Marine Regiment, recently redeployed from Shanghai to the Philippines. However, MacArthur's main plan was to use his PA divisions to stop any Japanese forces. MacArthur argued that the PA divisions would have a great motivation to defend their homeland as well as knowledge of the local area. Despite the lack of training, modern weapons, limited communications equipment, and scant transportation, the 11th and 21st Divisions faced a major Japanese invasion.

THE LINGAYEN GULF LANDINGS

The Lingayen Gulf area is on the west coast of the Philippines bordering the South China Sea. The eastern part of the gulf borders the Cordillera Central Mountains while the southern edge of the gulf abuts the Zambales Mountains. Homma intended to land and drive south between the Zambales and other mountain ranges along a valley that led directly to the Central Luzon plain, Manila, and victory.

Homma's 48th Division was the main attack force and an IJN force of three invasion fleets was launched from Formosa and the Pescadores. One invasion convoy left on December 18, the others a day later, for the planned landing on December 22. The IJN arrived in the early hours of December 22 with 76 Army and nine Navy transports. Additional naval forces, released from the Malaya campaign, protected the invasion fleet from any American aerial or naval threats.

While in transit to Lingayen area, the US Navy's SS-186 *Stingray* sighted the invasion fleet at 1313hrs on December 21, but it did not attack despite being ordered to do so. Hart sent six further submarines into the Lingayen Gulf, but only one submarine managed to sink a ship – *S-38* torpedoed the

Japanese landings along the Lingayen Gulf

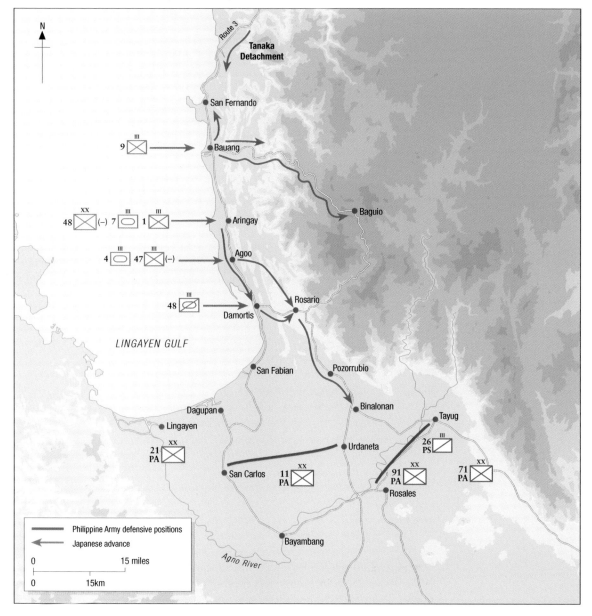

Japanese forces used propaganda leaflets like this one to get Americans or Filipinos to surrender. Some PA units suffered heavily from desertion, but most Americans and Filipinos fought to the end and went into Japanese captivity. (US Air Force)

transport *Hayo Maru* at about 0759hrs. This was one of the first victories by the Navy in the war, but it did not stop the invasion. The *Seal* also patrolled the area south of Vigan and she sank the 856-ton cargo ship *Hayataka Maru*. MacArthur complained to Hart about the Asiatic Fleet's poor submarine performance. Unfortunately, many of the torpedoes used in the early Pacific War had problems with their magnetic detonators and failed to work properly. Some torpedoes did not explode even after hitting their targets. The Navy's Mark XIV torpedo sank only two ships even though 66 were fired.

The IJA landing forces disembarked starting at about 0500hrs and continued throughout the day. The landing locations were at Agoo, Caba, and Bauang. Elements of the Tanaka Detachment that had earlier taken Aparri drove south along Route 3. Its mission was to reach the Lingayen Gulf invasion forces and support their drive to Manila. After seizing the Tuguegaro airfield, the Tanaka Detachment moved north back to the coast and then drove south past Vigan towards the Lingayen Gulf.

Japanese forces landed largely unopposed at their beaches. The few Filipino units that were present did not offer much resistance, though fire from 155mm field guns was heavy at times and caused many IJA casualties. Homma's 14th Army took Agoo with the 47th Infantry Regiment at 0517hrs. Up the coast, the 1st Formosa Regiment, artillery, and tanks landed near Caba, at Aringay, at 0530hrs. Later, at about 0730hrs, the northernmost landings occurred at Bauang with the 9th Infantry Regiment. This force, the Kamijima Detachment, was to link up with the Tanaka Detachment that was driving south. IJA personnel were also to land and seize Baguio as Homma feared that the Americans and the Filipinos might try to flank the Lingayen Gulf invasion force from there.

The Americans did offer some limited resistance with air and naval forces. An Australian-based B-17 force, which had bombed Davao earlier, was returning home when the four bombers strafed some of the escort ships without resulting in any major damage. P-40s joined the attack, though they too failed to stop or hinder any amphibious operations. Even Navy pilots flying PBYs tried to slow the Japanese, but they continued to stream ashore.

The Japanese drive into Luzon had several immediate goals. They needed to consolidate the beachheads, defeat any USAFFE defenses, move rapidly to seize several coastal cities, and start the drive southeast towards Manila. If the Japanese could break through the American defenses, then they could accomplish their 50-day goal of conquest. MacArthur's initial reports to Washington estimated upwards of 80,000 to 100,000 Japanese had landed in Luzon, an overstatement. Questionable PA units, limited American airpower, and scant naval forces might not hold out; MacArthur wanted reinforcements and aid immediately.

The 11th Division had set up some beach defenses at Bauang with .30- and .50-cal. machine guns causing heavy casualties in some IJA units. However, without artillery support, the Filipino units could not counter the IJA's Kamijima Detachment and they retreated. Many Filipino units simply ran at the sight of the Japanese.

The 71st Division also had units near the Bauang beaches. The Filipinos tried to meet the lead IJA units while flanking them near San Fernando. If all went well, they would smash Tanaka's 2nd Formosa Regiment. Unfortunately, the Kamijima Detachment moved faster than the PA estimated and elements of the IJA's 9th Infantry Regiment made contact with Tanaka's forces. Japanese units trapped parts of 11th and 71st Divisions between the Tanaka and Kamijima Detachments and the PA units had to withdraw through Baguio with Japanese forces hot on their tail.

The other landings occurred without incident and Japanese forces moved south on Route 3. Many 11th Division units also started to move south on Route 3 towards Damortis. Unless MacArthur and Wainwright could stop the advance, Homma would route the North Luzon Force. The only unit that was close and strong enough to slow the IJA Lingayen invasion force was the 26th Cavalry Regiment. The American-officered 26th Cavalry was one of the better units in the Philippines. Wainwright placed part of the unit north of Route 3, but an engagement with IJA tanks forced them to move to Damortis. Wainwright ordered more elements from the 26th Cavalry to defend Damortis, but by 1300hrs strong IJA and IJAAF attacks hit the Philippine Scouts hard and they also retreated.

Wainwright needed additional mobility to resist the Japanese, and Company C, 192nd Tank Battalion, moved to engage the enemy near Agoo. Company C could only send a five-tank platoon with a full fuel load since the battalion did not have sufficient gasoline resupply. IJAAF bombers failed to stop the tanks and the platoon moved towards Agoo. The M3s met IJA Type 95 light tanks and a Japanese round hit the lead American tank and set it on fire; its crew became the first American captives of the war. Under fire from the Japanese, the other four tanks moved south towards Rosario. These tanks became victims of IJAAF bombers the next day.

Major General Edward King commanded the Luzon Force late in the campaign and surrendered after the Japanese swept his defenders down the Bataan Peninsula. Here King surrenders to Colonel Nakayama Motoo. Homma was angry when he found out the only forces that gave up were those on Luzon, not all of the Philippines. (US Air Force)

IJA infantry units did not typically have access to motorized transportation, or even major roads, during the fight for Bataan. Japanese soldiers moved against the Americans through thick, steamy jungles. They carried artillery pieces and heavy equipment over rough terrain as depicted by a Japanese artist. (US Army)

By night, the Japanese pushed the Americans and Filipinos out of the immediate Lingayen Gulf area. One of the few units not to break ranks against the Japanese was the 26th Cavalry. Taking many casualties, the cavalrymen contested the advancing IJA. Despite fighting against Japanese tanks, the 26th Cavalry held at Binalonan on December 24. Holding the town for a few hours allowed other PA units to move south, and the Philippine Scout cavalry held until the afternoon when they abandoned it to Homma's forces. In late November 1941, the 26th Cavalry had 842 officers and men; it now only had 450 in its ranks. However, the PA units still could not stop the IJA and Japanese units soon took Rosario.

The only force under Wainwright's direct command to cover any retreat was his weakened 26th Cavalry and, along with the remnants of the 192nd Tank Battalion, they again tried to delay the Japanese in Rosario to allow the other PA divisions to reorganize and establish defensive positions. However, the IJA units continued their moves south and east and the Japanese armor proved too much for the defenders and they too had to move to Pozorrubio. MacArthur's planned active defense operations to stop the Japanese on the beaches had failed. The Japanese seemed in position to move towards Manila uncontested along Route 3. All MacArthur could hope for was that Washington could meet his request for immediate reinforcements. MacArthur had no choice but to establish stronger defensive positions or Homma would overrun the PA.

Between December 22 and 28, Homma managed to land 43,110 men in the Philippines at Lingayen. The 14th Army sent in 34,856 soldiers with the remaining personnel coming from naval and air forces. Bad weather, heavy seas, and damaged landing craft delayed, but did not stop the landings. These enemy numbers were far smaller than MacArthur's initial estimates that had inflated the Lingayen force alone to upwards of 100,000 men. The pre-war American Army military strength was 31,095, which included FEAF and recently deployed reinforcements from the United States. Total mobilized PA personnel numbered around 120,000 (not all on Luzon). Although the Filipino soldiers far outnumbered the IJA, they were not ready to meet the Japanese on an equal footing.

"WPO-3 IS IN EFFECT"

The immediate need was to stop the Japanese before the entire American-Filipino force faced a rout. The Japanese pushed the Filipino forces past Pozorrubio; they seemed beaten. One obstacle that could delay the IJA's 48th Division was the Agno River. General MacArthur now had to reevaluate his position on WPO-3 and he decided to implement it. Wainwright requested approval to create a defensive position behind the Agno. This "defensive" line was the first of five planned, their purpose being to delay the advancement while the PA moved into Bataan and prepare for a contracted defense. MacArthur's staff had pre-planned and practiced manning these defensive actions before the war. The first four defensive lines, D-1 to D-4, would provide a token resistance, just enough to slow down the Japanese advance. American-Filipino forces would then have sufficient time to prepare the last defensive position, D-5, and a heavier resistance. Mountain ranges east and west anchored this position with Fort Stotsenburg, Mount Arayat, and the Candara Swamps in between the D-5 position. At the D-5 line, the American-Filipino force was to hold the Japanese long enough for the South Luzon Force and units near Manila to retreat into Bataan. Wainwright also needed more troops and he requested the Philippine Division from MacArthur; this request was denied.

The raw PA reserve divisions could not stand up against the IJA. IJAAF and IJNAF aircraft ruled the skies; there was little hope of using the FEAF consistently to counter any Japanese offensives. The Navy had largely moved out of the Philippines and the IJN could operate with relative impunity. For the Americans, Christmas Eve would see a change in strategy, the crumbling of the North Luzon Force, a major Japanese invasion south of Manila, and few aircraft in the area. The remaining FEAF P-40s and other aircraft flew south to Mindanao or Bataan from where they were able to conduct only limited reconnaissance, strafing, and bombing. The one saving grace for MacArthur was the dispatch of a resupply convoy built around the cruiser *Pensacola*. This had left the West Coast shortly before December 7.

The *Pensacola* convoy contained P-40 and A-24 aircraft, artillery, munitions, and other supplies. Whilst it was underway an old argument resurfaced in the War and Navy Departments. The Army and Navy war planners now believed the convoy should divert from going to MacArthur and reinforce Hawaii. Hawaii was more important strategically than the Philippines, and many in Washington believed that MacArthur's forces were already doomed. Roosevelt, Secretary of War Henry Stimson, and Marshall, however, decided to provide MacArthur with some reinforcements in order to boost morale and the decision was taken to sail the convoy to Brisbane, Australia. From there, American officials could try to send it through to the Philippines. Unfortunately, attempts to supply MacArthur's forces largely failed. Some limited supplies reached the Philippines via submarine, blockade-runners, and aircraft. However, only three P-40Es from Australia reached Mindanao during the campaign.

MacArthur's original defense plans had included placing supplies and maintenance depots close to potential invasion sites; however, the Bataan Peninsula had been overlooked. The fortresses in Manila Bay, like Corregidor, had stocks of food and ammunition, but the approved WPO-3 retreat area of Bataan had fewer reserves. The rapid IJA advance and American change of strategy created huge problems for American logisticians. They needed to supply troops in transit while building a stockpile for Bataan. Difficult terrain and limited ground transport also contributed to the problems in preparing Bataan's defenses. However, Japanese units would also have to move slowly through thick jungles and mountainous areas, with few roads, in Bataan.

THE JAPANESE STRIKE AT LAMON BAY

In the early hours of December 24 the 16th Division prepared to strike at Lamon Bay. The invasion fleet had left the Ryukus on December 17 with 24 transport vessels. About 7,000 IJA soldiers disembarked at three locations: Japanese landing craft came ashore at Mauban, Atimonan, and Siain. Facing the Japanese were elements of the 1st Regular Division, the only regular PA unit, and the 51st Division. The IJA 16th Division was not at full strength as some of their forces had taken Legaspi. Stationed and fighting in China, the 16th Division did not have a sterling combat reputation. Once ashore, the 16th Division was supposed to link up with the Kimura Detachment moving up from Legaspi. Homma could now put pressure on MacArthur on two fronts and perhaps even trap the Americans in a pincer movement.

The Lamon Bay defenders lacked artillery and direct-fire support weapons to stem the Japanese. The 51st Division had earlier received orders to move south against any Kimura Detachment movement. However, on the public release of the shift to WPO-3, Brigadier General Albert Jones, the new South Luzon Force commander, had contacted his commanders to start pulling out of the Bichol Peninsula. MacArthur had earlier ordered Parker to Bataan to develop its defensive positions. If the Japanese moved against Lamon Bay, then they would have mountainous terrain to overcome as they drove on to Manila. Jones' troops could delay their advance to the capital with an aggressive fighting withdrawal.

The 16th Division's units that landed opposite the 1st Regular Division faced stiff resistance. The Filipino division had dug in around the Mauban area to await any Japanese landing and at dawn, when the IJA's 20th Infantry

The IJA's 14th Army expected a major fight to take Manila. MacArthur believed that any defense of the Philippine capital was useless and moved his forces to Bataan. Japanese forces then advanced unopposed into Manila and the city escaped destruction and major civilian casualties. (Tom Laemlein/Armor Plate Press)

Japanese landings at Lamon Bay

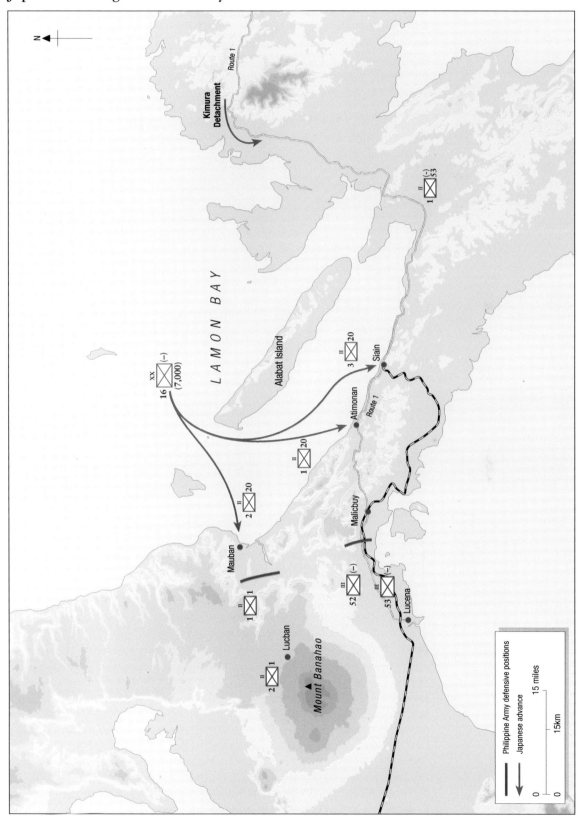

they met heavy resistance and suffered heavy casualties before they were able to push the defenders back. American P-40 and P-35 fighters supported the Filipinos, but were unable to make much of a difference. IJA forces landing on other beaches faced slender resistance and were able to join up with units from Legaspi that had moved along the Bichol Peninsula.

Japanese reconnaissance units at Mauban pushed west to bypass the Lamon Bay defenders and tried to find paths around Mount Banahao. Other 16th Division units pressed westward to reach Tayabas Bay and force the 52nd Division out of Route 1, the main road leading to Manila to the northwest. The bulk of the 16th Division planned to move across the Tayabas Mountains, continue on Route 1, pass Cavite, and on to Manila. Homma realized that by Christmas Eve his forces were in position to capture Manila. The Lingayen invasion force pushed the PA divisions back at every encounter. The 48th Division was only about 100 miles from Manila while the 16th Division was even closer to the capital. Victory, in Homma's eyes, seemed in sight.

MacArthur's shift to WPO-3 also included the forces on South Luzon. Coordination between the North and South Luzon Forces had to be precise when it came to moving to Bataan; if one force retreated too fast, then the other might face the Japanese alone and could be annihilated. Like the North Luzon Force, Jones had to delay the Japanese advance as PA units slowly pulled back across the coast towards Mount Banahao. The 1st Regular Division tried to hinder Homma's advance towards Los Banos, while the 51st Division covered the area south of Mount Banahao, linking up with the 1st Regular Division close to Los Banos. The only mobile force available to the Filipinos was Company C, 194th Tank Battalion. Although the combined American-Filipino force had more personnel than the 16th Division, the Japanese advanced to Los Banos on December 28, and the following day the 51st Division sent some of its units into Bataan.

THE RETREAT TO BATAAN

Despite MacArthur's soldiers' best efforts, there was little hope that the American-Filipino forces could hold onto Manila. If MacArthur attempted to defend the capital he could lose his entire force. The PA divisions had crumbled under the Japanese advance. Thousands of civilians might die and the Japanese destroy the city through an extended fight. Instead, MacArthur had informed Marshall, in a December 22 radio message, that he had decided to declare Manila an open city. His headquarters and the Philippine government would move to Corregidor.

One of the most critical issues facing the defenders was to move supplies into Bataan for its defense. Depots around the Philippines started to remove supplies for movement into Bataan. However, the hurried retreat caused the abandonment of much needed items that fell into the hands of the advancing Japanese Army. At Fort Stotsenburg, logistics officers reportedly left 250,000 out of 300,000 gallons of gasoline, warehouses of supplies, and some damaged aircraft. Similarly, troops left the depots at Tarlac and Los Baños, though other retreating units managed to destroy the supplies. Threats of court-martial barred any American officers from confiscating 2,000 cases of canned goods and clothing owned by Japanese wholesalers. MacArthur's logistical officers had moved 18,000 tons of supplies close to the Lingayen Gulf in anticipation of the Japanese invasion at advanced depots and

American and Filipino soldiers, airmen, Marines, and sailors defended Bataan used a variety of weapons and equipment. This American captain has a .45-cal. Thompson submachine gun. The Filipino soldier has a revolver on his left hip and possibly a .45-cal. M1911 automatic pistol on his right. (Tom Laemlein/Armor Plate Press)

railheads. Unfortunately, moving supplies back to Bataan was difficult as transportation was limited. PA units had commandeered vehicles to retreat, not take supplies. At Cabanatuan, the Americans left 50 million bushels of rice, a five-year supply, to the Japanese. Allegedly, Quezon had persuaded MacArthur not to take the food, but leave it in place.

Logistics officers had based their planning on a much smaller number of soldiers than actually turned up in the Bataan Peninsula. MacArthur's decision to put WPO-3 into operation directed many PA units and other forces onto Bataan. These included the Philippine Division, FEAF personnel that did not have aircraft to send into combat, naval personnel stranded in Olongapo and Cavite, and civilians grasping at any avenue to escape the Japanese. More personnel than planned and the failure to develop appropriate logistics was another problem for MacArthur's forces.

Wainwright still had a critical role to play for MacArthur – he had to keep the roads open to Manila and other areas to allow the buildup of supplies and troops into Bataan. Filipino units were compelled to shift their positions rapidly in the face of frontal or flanking Japanese attacks, and this left Wainwright with little time to develop any substantial fortifications or defensive positions. Their only concern was to slow Homma and the 48th Division while other assigned forces prepared positions in Bataan.

From December 24 to 31, Wainwright's PA divisions managed to stall the 48th Division in the Central Luzon plain. The PA had three divisions (11th, 21st, and 91st, plus the weakened 26th Cavalry Regiment) and the American Provisional Tank Group of two M3 tank battalions to cover the retreat. American and PA engineers created obstacles across roads and destroyed key bridges.

American forces had limited mobile forces to plug any gaps in their defenses or cover retreating units. The American tanks and halftracks armed with 75mm guns were the only mobile reserve available to the defenders. They allowed the PA units to move south while the tanks formed roadblocks on Route 3. Unfortunately, the coordination between the tank group and the

Manila area defenses

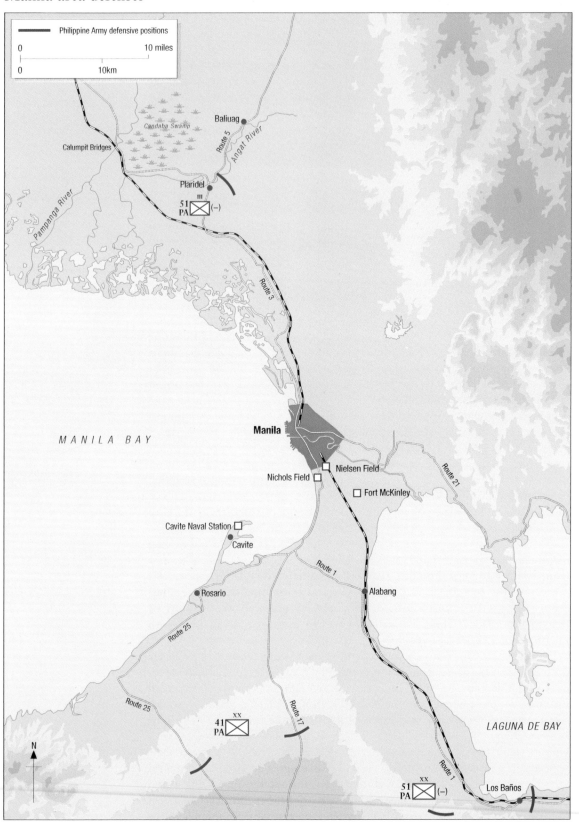

PA units was lacking. One situation resulted in several lost tanks. While moving south of Moncada, 15 M3 Stuart tank crews had to abandon their vehicles since they discovered engineers had destroyed the bridges over an impassable stream before they could cross it.

Japanese commanders concentrated against two areas to break through the heavily defended Agno River line. The IJA's 9th Reconnaissance and 1st Formosa Regiments attempted a break through at Carmen against the 11th Division. Meanwhile, the rest of Homma's 48th Division hit the battered 26th Cavalry Regiment at Tayug. Once the Japanese had created a hole in the cavalry's position, Japanese tanks could exploit the opening and break out southwards along Route 3. If the Japanese could drive rapidly down Route 5, then Homma's forces might entrap the PA divisions before pushing on to Calumpit and capturing the bridges over the Pampanga River. The Americans and Filipinos also needed to keep the Calumpit bridges open to maintain a link to Manila to allow supplies and forces to move from south Luzon to Bataan. Another key city for the Americans was San Fernando in central Luzon. This was located near an important road junction between Route 3 and Route 7, the main road to Bataan. On December 26 American officials declared Manila an open city, with MacArthur pulling all his units out of the city by 31 December. This status made the Japanese realize that they would need to advance to Bataan to deliver a decisive blow against MacArthur. Homma also had to occupy and administer Manila, which would divert some of his limited forces and upset his timetable for conquest. Homma's 48th Division also had to stop any reinforcements and supplies entering Bataan; this meant the capture of San Fernando and the destruction of the Calumpit bridges. Plaridel, south of Baliuag, was another vital road junction that the Japanese needed to capture. This town controlled roads towards Calumpit and Manila. Homma sent the 48th Division's 7th Tank Regiment and engineers to capture and repair any bridges leading to these targets and remove any demolitions. The Sonoda Force, named after the 7th Tank Regiment's commander, moved fast to capture the bridges and road junctions.

Filipino forces hurried from the South Luzon Force up along Route 3 to hold Calumpit and the area around the Pampanga River. The 51st Division, who had not been in combat, and the 194th Tank Battalion moved north to thwart any Japanese move to capture the Calumpit bridges. IJA forces moving south had pushed the 91st Division steadily towards the junction of Routes 3 and 5. The 91st Division had taken a beating from the IJA's Lingayen Gulf forces. Wainwright now ordered the 71st Division to bolster the 91st. Japanese troops had reached the outskirts of Baliuag on the last day of December and threatened to reach Route 3 and cut off access for the South Luzon Force and Manila to Bataan.

The Sonoda Force's tanks reached Baliuag without major resistance early on December 31. Filipino soldiers had destroyed a bridge north of the town but that did not stop the advance south. While Japanese engineers attempted to fix the bridge, the 71st Division's artillery fired on the Japanese forces. PA soldiers held the town, but soon started a withdrawal towards Plaridel. Stuart tanks had established a defensive position and fired on the Japanese tanks with the M3s forcing the Japanese armor back.

Jones discovered that his officers had prematurely ordered the 71st Division to leave Baliuag. Instead of leaving the IJA to the 51st Division holding Plaridel, Jones sent in two tank platoons and six halftracks against the Japanese. The tanks entered Baliuag's eastern side while Filipino artillery

Mitsubishi Sally bombers fly over Corregidor to pummel the island. These planes had a range of about 1,678 miles while carrying a 2,205-pound bomb load. At this point of the campaign, there was little FEAF opposition to the IJAAF or IJNAF. (US Army)

fire smashed into the town and provided some cover for the tanks' advance. The American armor engaged Japanese tank and infantry units in Baliuag at about 1700hrs, disrupting the Sonoda Force and creating time for the PA divisions and other units to get across the Pampanga River safely. The M3 Stuarts inflicted eight Japanese losses without any in return.

On New Year's Day the last of the South Luzon Force moved past Calumpit. Jones had successfully pulled out his forces by 0500hrs. The only task left was to blow the twin bridges over the Pampanga River. Japanese officers in the 48th Division had urged destruction of the Calumpit bridges earlier to trap the PA units, but the IJAAF had resisted. With little air opposition, the IJAAF could have sealed any retreat route for the South Luzon Force by destroying the spans. Wainwright, who was now in command following the merger of the North and South Luzon Forces into the Bataan Force, ordered the bridges blown at 0615hrs.

The North Luzon Force and other units now had to hold the area near San Fernando. Units in the defensive line D-5 held the Japanese above San Fernando with Filipino soldiers from the 11th and 21st Division stretched across the Bamban River on January 1. Homma concentrated an infantry regiment, the Kanno Detachment, and artillery units to break through the 21st Division. Filipino soldiers had already destroyed two bridges that crossed the river, but the Japanese appeared ready to move south. Although delayed by the defenders, the PA divisions started to move towards Bataan. The rail and road junctions passing through San Fernando lost their importance with the destruction of the Calumpit bridges.

Japanese units had followed the Filipinos south, taking Clark Field while the PA divisions established a new defensive line south of San Fernando. Any delays by Homma would allow Parker to make additional preparations for an IJA assault into Bataan. By January 2, despite the destroyed bridges, IJA units had crossed the Pampanga River at Calumpit and moved north along Route 3. The 48th Division concentrated on the battered 11th and 21st Divisions holding the entrance to Bataan.

From New Year's Day until January 6, the 11th and 21st Divisions withdrew towards Layac where they formed a new defensive line. Artillery fire helped hold the defensive line. Constant Japanese attacks hammered the PA units and slowly forced the defenders back. Fortunately, the American tanks and the 26th Cavalry Regiment managed to stem the Japanese advance and the IJA were taking heavy casualties. For example, the Tanaka Detachment tried to capture the town of Gaugua on the early morning of January 5. Under full moonlight, the detachment attacked Filipino positions across an open field and road and was decimated by artillery fire. Despite repeated attempts to capture the town, the unit suffered so many casualties that it had to be replaced at daybreak. The 26th Cavalry, American tanks, and the remnants of the 11th and 21st Divisions stood between Homma and the rest of Wainwright and Parker's forces across an 8-mile neck behind the Cuto River. A steel bridge over the Cuto River at Layac now served as another chokepoint against Homma's advance. The remainder of the North Luzon Force had pushed south and withdrawn into Bataan. The 26th Cavalry pulled out at 0700hrs on January 7 for Bataan as MacArthur left central Luzon to the Japanese.

One lucky act for MacArthur was an IGHQ decision to use the 48th Division to support the Netherlands East Indies campaign, a decision taken before the start of the Philippines campaign. With Homma's best division gone, MacArthur's defenders had a chance to stop the Japanese. After the fall of Manila on January 2, Homma now established his headquarters in the capital. He now had to rely on the 16th Division and the 65th Independent Mixed Brigade for the rest of the campaign. The 65th Brigade was not a first-line combat unit, instead consisting of mobilized reservists. The brigade was more appropriate for occupation duties rather than active fighting in Bataan.

Homma expected the beaten Americans and Filipinos to fold in the face of his IJA forces. MacArthur had lost about 13,000 men since the Lingayen Gulf and Lamon Bay landings while Homma's casualties numbered about 2,000. Many PA divisions had also suffered widespread desertions. The Americans and Filipinos had not put up significant resistance to the Japanese offensive and, at best, they could only retreat to Corregidor where the Japanese could shell and bomb at will, starve the defenders, and finally invade the fortress. There was no major FEAF or Asiatic Fleet opposition to worry the Japanese; it was still possible to achieve the 50-day conquest of the Philippines.

BATAAN: THE FINAL REFUGE

Bataan was a fine defensive location. The peninsula only had two main north–south roads on each coast and one road that bisected it. The eastern coast had a wider maneuver area, at least near the base of the peninsula. Bataan was about 25 miles long and about 15 miles wide at its center and dominated by several mountain ranges. Corregidor was located off the southern coast of the peninsula. The vegetation was mostly jungle and, if the defenders could entrench their positions, then the Japanese might not find the capture of Bataan as easy as their landings at Lingayen Gulf or Lamon Bay. However, the defenders had major logistical concerns. Limited supplies of food, medicine, weapons, and ammunition put the defenders in a perilous position. The planners of WPO-3 had assumed the Pacific Fleet would rescue the defenders in six months – an improbable timetable. Given the limited food supply, MacArthur's logisticians put all Army personnel on half rations on January 5. Army officers had planned on feeding and supporting about 43,000 military personnel. Instead, the American and Filipino force now numbered over 80,000 soldiers and 26,000 civilians.

THE FIGHT AT BALIUAG (pp. 58–59)

On December 31, 1941, Company C, 192nd Tank Battalion, attacked Japanese tanks in the streets of Baliuag. Japanese advances down Route 5 threatened to cut off American and Filipino access through Route 3 to the Calumpit Bridges. If Homma's forces succeeded then it would be impossible to retreat from Manila into Bataan, and Japanese units could then defeat American or Filipino units in detail. Elements of the Philippine Army's 71st and 91st Divisions held a defensive position near the town of Baliuag and if the Americans and Filipinos could hold the town then they could prevent the Japanese from taking the Calumpit Bridges and occupying Route 3. On December 31 Japanese armor appeared east of the town around 1330hrs. By 1500hrs, the main Japanese column had reached Baliuag and was ready to attack the 71st and 91st Divisions, as well as the untested 51st Division. Brigadier

General Albert Jones, commanding the region around Baliuag, ordered the only available mobile force, the 192nd Tank Battalion, to engage the Japanese Sonoda Force. At 1700hrs, two M3 Stuart tank (1) platoons, supported by M3 halftracks carrying 75mm howitzers, crossed the Angat River to engage Japanese forces in the town. The tanks fought in the streets among a mix of buildings and Nipa huts (2). The American tankers, mobilized Army National Guardsmen, encountered medium tanks from the Japanese 7th Tank Regiment. The Japanese used Type 89 medium tanks (3). In this action, the Japanese lost eight tanks. The Type 89 had a 57mm gun, but fired only high-explosive shells, not armor-piercing ones. Some American tankers reported the Japanese rounds bouncing off their tanks. There were no American losses and the attack was a complete success.

Filipino military forces required additional training during the campaign. Here, USMC instructors demonstrate how to use a Browning .30-cal. machine gun. The Filipino aviation cadets shown here were pressed into service as infantry duty owing to the destruction of MacArthur's air forces. (DOD)

MacArthur split his forces in Bataan into two corps. Wainwright was to command I Philippine Corps of 22,500 personnel covering the western part of Bataan. I Corps had four PA divisions, the 1st, 31st, 71st, and the 91st Divisions, and the 26th Cavalry Regiment. Parker led the II Philippine Corps that covered the eastern half of Bataan with 25,000 soldiers. He had also four PA divisions (11th, 21st, 41st, and 51st) plus the 57th Infantry Regiment (PS) from the Philippine Division.

MacArthur created three main areas of operation: Wainwright and Parker defended a main battle position based around Mounts Silanganan and Natib in the center of the line. Natib had a 4,222ft peak and American officers thought the steep and rugged mountainous area impossible to traverse. This position started at the edge of the South China Sea at Mauban and ran 4 miles east to Mount Silanganan. Wainwright's I Corps defended this position, known as the Mauban Line. The position then extended from Mount Natib's foothills to Mabatang on Manila Bay's shore near Abucay, and troops from II Corps covered this section known as the Abucay Line. Since MacArthur's staff assumed that Mount Natib was impenetrable, the Americans did not extend the main battle position so that I and II Corps met in the middle. The unguarded, but patrolled, gaps would provide the Japanese with an avenue of advance against the Americans and the Filipinos.

MacArthur also formed a rear battle position that stretched from Bagac to Orion across the peninsula, about 8 miles south of the main battle position, based around Mount Samat. Under WPO-3, this position was supposed to have acted as the main line of resistance but it gave little room for the defenders to move. This rear battle position was the last chance for MacArthur to defend Bataan.

A service command area was at the tip of the peninsula near the Mariveles Mountains from where support personnel provided supply and maintenance help to the forward positions. This area was under threat from a Japanese amphibious assault along the shoreline from Manila Bay to Mariveles, a port that supported Corregidor. The defending forces included the Philippine Constabulary, the 4th Marines, FEAF, and naval personnel.

The IJA advanced south in Bataan across wide jungles and over steep mountains. Though slowed by enemy opposition, disease, and physical obstacles, the Japanese struggled through, though they had to rely on reinforcements to eventually defeat Wainwright's forces on Bataan. (US Army)

MacArthur's strategy was to conduct a defense in depth, taking advantage of the rugged terrain to fend off the Japanese until reinforcements arrived. It was most probable that Homma would attack on the east coast of Bataan since the only usable road, Route 110 (the East Road), connected with Route 7 and the Japanese forces now north of Bataan. The coastal plain on the east coast also provided maneuver room for the Japanese. The west coast did not have a road connection north and the Japanese would require time to cut through jungles.

After pushing the Americans and Filipinos out of Luzon, IJA forces had to reorganize and prepare for their final move into Bataan. Nara, the 65th Brigade commander, pushed south on the East Road with three infantry regiments (9th, 141st, and 142nd) and the 7th Tank Regiment to break the II Philippine Corps' position. Each of the infantry regiments formed regimental combat teams with supporting units and attempted to breach the main battle position supported by heavy artillery fire. Nara's force was to drive across the foothills of Mount Natib across to the eastern coastal plain. The other regimental combat teams would also try to penetrate the defensive lines on the East Road and along the coastal plain.

Using jungle trails, a single regimental combat team moved south on the west coast of Bataan. The IJA's 122nd Regiment was to first move west along Route 7 then to Olongapo and finally Bagac, which was the start of the only lateral road crossing Bataan. This part of the offensive would take time as there were no suitable roads in this area.

Facing Nara's main thrust near the Abucay Hacienda was the 51st Division. As a part of the South Luzon Force the division had failed to stop the 16th Division at Lamon Bay, and holding the edge of II Corps' defensive line seemed a quiet reserve position for the tired division. The 41st Division held the center of the line and its best-trained and equipped unit was the 57th Infantry Regiment which was entering combat for the first time. This unit held the East Road near Mabatang.

THE JAPANESE BREAK THE ABUCAY AND MAUBAN LINES

On January 9 Nara started moving against the Abucay Line. Two Japanese regimental combat teams advanced across the defensive positions previously held by MacArthur's men at the neck of the Bataan Peninsula and moved south along the East Road at 1500hrs. This advance was carried out under heavy artillery fire as American artillery observers had used the opportunity to survey the East Road carefully. Advance Japanese units skirmished with Philippine Scouts, but no major confrontation occurred. Meanwhile, the Japanese 122nd Infantry Regiment moved west to Olongapo without opposition, though it encountered destroyed bridges and mines that slowed their advance. The Japanese captured Fort Wint, a coastal defense position (like Corregidor), and then Olongapo.

The following day, the main attack started against the Abucay Line. Japanese forces advanced in good order in the western sector of the Abucay Line but were heavily targeted by Parker's artillery, and Nara pushed most of the 141st Infantry Regiment further west to avoid this fire.

With the Japanese ready to hit the Abucay Line, MacArthur decided to visit his forces on Bataan. Travelling by PT boat to Mariveles from his headquarters on Corregidor he conferred with Parker and Wainwright. During his stay on Bataan he came under Japanese artillery fire, but refused to take cover. Although he showed personal courage in this instance, this was his only trip to Bataan during the campaign. To bolster the morale of his troops MacArthur continued to tell his commanders that more aid was on the way, though nearly all of the officers and men on Bataan knew this was unlikely. Around this time a Japanese plane delivered Homma's first demand for MacArthur's surrender; the American response was heavier shelling of Nara's forces.

Japanese elements of the 2nd Battalion, 141st Infantry Regiment, started to cross the Calaguiman River against the Abucay Line on the night of January 11 against the positions of the 57th Infantry. These night attacks failed to break through the Filipino positions and resulted in heavy casualties. Eventually, by the 12th, Nara's forces made some headway, but Filipino counterattacks regained most of the lost territory. Despite the concerted effort to push out the defenders, Nara's forces had a tough fight on their hands as Parker poured in more reserves around Matabang.

Nara did have some successes against the middle and western sectors of the Abucay Line. In the center Japanese efforts pushed the 41st Division back, but the Filipinos did not break. The far western sector of the Abucay Line was another story. The battered 51st Division received repeated attacks, and only counterattacks by reserve forces saved the line from crumbling totally. Heavy Japanese artillery and air attacks took their toll on the defenders and the continual pressure on the 51st Division had the desired effect. Units from Nara's 141st Infantry Regiment found a seam between the 41st and 51st Divisions on January 15 and Japanese units began to peel back the 51st Division along the Abucay Line. Parker had already committed all of his reserves and none remained. The Japanese 9th Infantry Regiment, which had moved west, was now ready to turn the flank on the Abucay Line.

Parker's entire defensive position was now in serious trouble. He ordered a counterattack by the 51st Division, with reinforcements from the 21st Division, despite protests by its commander. This counterattack kicked off early on January 16 and managed to push back the Japanese. However, Nara had anticipated such a move and planned to use the 9th Regiment to envelop the Filipinos once they had advanced; the 51st Division started to collapse rapidly.

MacArthur had to fill the breach. If the attack failed then the entire main battle position might disintegrate. Another threat that MacArthur faced was Japanese columns advancing into the I Corps area. By January 16, the 122nd Infantry Regiment had moved south from Olongapo and was approaching Moron. The 26th Cavalry Regiment engaged the Japanese near Moron on that day when they made the last known horse-mounted charge of World War II. They and PA infantry scattered the Japanese troops as they tried to cross the Batalan River. However, under heavy pressure Wainwright's men had to withdraw from Moron on the 17th.

The Abucay Line was still MacArthur's main concern and he ordered the Philippine Division and other reserves to plug the gap left by the 51st Division. Nara prepared to slice through the Abucay Line along the Abo Abo River valley using the 9th Infantry Regiment. The American 31st Infantry Regiment and 45th Infantry Regiment (PS) tried to stem the Japanese advance around Abucay Hacienda, but they could not hold them.

Nara and Parker's forces collided in a series of attacks and counterattacks, without a decisive action. It was possible that Parker might be able to hold on, but Homma continued to press the American-Filipino positions. Nara prepared a massive assault for January 22 to break through the Philippine Division and push through the Abucay Line.

Sutherland and others recognized that the Japanese could exploit the center of the main battle positions and come through the Mount Natib area, but Wainwright still believed the route near Mount Natib was impassable and I Corps safe. However, Wainwright's beliefs about the terrain were wrong and IJA forces used the "impassable" terrain to move against the defensive positions. Homma demanded more progress against I Corps and he enlisted the 16th Division's 20th Infantry Regiment plus artillery and antitank units, and the Kimura Detachment from the Davao landing. Effectively, Kimura was now in charge of the assault on the I Corps area on January 18, leaving Nara to concentrate on the fight against II Corps.

Kimura's forces started to push the 1st Regular Division units out of the Mauban Line. Moving unopposed to the east, Kimura managed to break through and he drove southwest from the Silanganan ridge and cut off the defenders of the Mauban Line. By January 21, the 20th Regiment had broken through the line in force and Japanese soldiers had blocked the West Road enveloping elements of the 1st Regular Division units while other IJA units pushed towards the coast. All attempts to relieve the roadblock failed and lack of food, supplies, and ammunition forced the American and Filipino forces to retreat.

On the Abucay Line, Nara's January 22 offensive began with a heavy artillery barrage. Parker's men were also short of rations and other supplies, and hunger started to degrade their combat capability. Japanese air units pounded the Americans and Filipinos and IJAAF bombers prevented any defensive artillery. Under this relentless pressure, the defenders were pushed out of the Abucay Hacienda.

MacArthur began to receive reports about the deteriorating position along the main battle position: counterattacks along the Abucay Line were floundering, while the Mauban Line was also under increasing pressure from

Kimura's advance. On January 22, MacArthur decided to pull all remaining units out of the entire main battle positions starting on the evening of January 23. Wainwright and Parker would have to retreat or face a rout. The American and Filipino forces planned to move south down the sole road bisecting Bataan, the Bagac–Pilar road. All units had to be in position in the new defensive line by January 26.

The Abucay–Mauban Line started to crumble rapidly. On the Mauban Line, units retreated south with any vehicles, heavy weapons, equipment, and supplies not able to be moved out of the line being destroyed. In the Abucay Line the Philippine Division and PA reinforcements also began to pull back.

By January 26, all I and II Corps units had left their defensive positions and were now in the rear battle position, the Bagac–Orion Line. This line was continuous and offered MacArthur a better chance of fending off Japanese attacks. Each corps area of responsibility was divided into sectors, with divisions assigned to them to prevent a Japanese breakthrough, though these units had been worn down by the continual fighting.

THE BATTLE FOR THE POINTS

Japanese forces had succeeded in punching through the Mauban Line, but it had taken time. The next target was the city and naval base of Mariveles, which would open the way to Corregidor. In order to avoid the difficult terrain, bypass the American defenses, and sever the West Road Homma planned an amphibious operation. This move would also slice Wainwright's communications and supply routes. Kimura and his staff planned to use the 1st and 2nd Battalions from the 20th Infantry Regiment for the landings.

The Japanese soldiers would have to land in small, isolated inlets and then fight their way over sharp cliffs and points rising from the sea. These units would operate independently with little chance of reinforcement until Kimura could puncture the main defenses. One battalion would depart from Moron and the other would serve as a reserve based in Olongapo to reinforce the amphibious force if they had faced problems. Kimura's plan was to send the 2nd Battalion in landing craft south of Bagac near Caibobo Point. If the landing was successful then it might compel the American commanders to pull out of Bagac or suffer defeat. The landing craft set out from Moron on the evening of January 22.

Unfortunately for Kimura the landings went awry. Japanese sailors faced rough seas, poor weather, American PT boats, and suffered from poor-quality maps. The bad weather and high seas disoriented the landing craft crews, while during the night *PT-34* sank two of the landing craft. The only maps available to Kimura's forces were large-scale maps that were not suitable for navigation, particularly at night. This was recurring problem for Homma's forces throughout the campaign. Japanese sailors also misidentified the landing zone, coming ashore at Quinauan Point, about 4 miles south of their target Caibobo Point. Another part of the battalion landed at Longoskawayan Point even further south, 7 miles down the coast from Quinauan Point. From here, the Japanese forces had less than a mile to drive into Mariveles but they were very isolated.

The only American and Filipino troops defending this area were a mixed force of FEAF airmen, Marines, sailors, and Philippine Constabulary and many of these defenders only had rudimentary training as infantry. Near

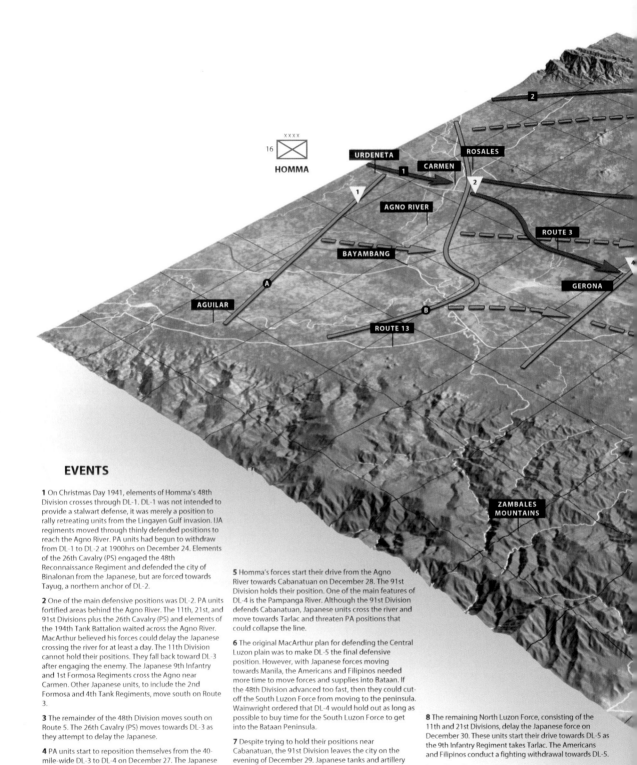

EVENTS

1 On Christmas Day 1941, elements of Homma's 48th Division crosses through DL-1. DL-1 was not intended to provide a stalwart defense, it was merely a position to rally retreating units from the Lingayen Gulf invasion. IJA regiments moved through thinly defended positions to reach the Agno River. PA units had begun to withdraw from DL-1 to DL-2 at 1900hrs on December 24. Elements of the 26th Cavalry (PS) engaged the 48th Reconnaissance Regiment and defended the city of Binalonan from the Japanese, but are forced towards Tayug, a northern anchor of DL-2.

2 One of the main defensive positions was DL-2. PA units fortified areas behind the Agno River. The 11th, 21st, and 91st Divisions plus the 26th Cavalry (PS) and elements of the 194th Tank Battalion waited across the Agno River. MacArthur believed his forces could delay the Japanese crossing the river for at least a day. The 11th Division cannot hold their positions. They fall back toward DL-3 after engaging the enemy. The Japanese 9th Infantry and 1st Formosa Regiments cross the Agno near Carmen. Other Japanese units, to include the 2nd Formosa and 4th Tank Regiments, move south on Route 3.

3 The remainder of the 48th Division moves south on Route 5. The 26th Cavalry (PS) moves towards DL-3 as they attempt to delay the Japanese.

4 PA units start to reposition themselves from the 40-mile-wide DL-3 to DL-4 on December 27. The Japanese require time to consolidate their gains and reorganize. Elements of the American 194th Tank Battalion use their M3 Stuart tanks to thwart Japanese advances and allow the Americans and Filipinos to maneuver into their new locations.

5 Homma's forces start their drive from the Agno River towards Cabanatuan on December 28. The 91st Division holds their position. One of the main features of DL-4 is the Pampanga River. Although the 91st Division defends Cabanatuan, Japanese units cross the river and move towards Tarlac and threaten PA positions that could collapse the line.

6 The original MacArthur plan for defending the Central Luzon plain was to make DL-5 the final defensive position. However, with Japanese forces moving towards Manila, the Americans and Filipinos needed more time to move forces and supplies into Bataan. If the 48th Division advanced too fast, then they could cut-off the South Luzon Force from moving to the peninsula. Wainwright ordered that DL-4 would hold out as long as possible to buy time for the South Luzon Force to get into the Bataan Peninsula.

7 Despite trying to hold their positions near Cabanatuan, the 91st Division leaves the city on the evening of December 29. Japanese tanks and artillery support the IJA's 47th Infantry Regiment as it moves into Cabanatuan. The 91st Division follows Route 5 towards Baliuag. American M3 tanks also move towards Baliuag to ensure the Japanese do not capture the Calumpit bridges over the Pampanga River.

8 The remaining North Luzon Force, consisting of the 11th and 21st Divisions, delay the Japanese force on December 30. These units start their drive towards DL-5 as the 9th Infantry Regiment takes Tarlac. The Americans and Filipinos conduct a fighting withdrawal towards DL-5.

9 Final North Luzon Force positions at DL-5 on December 31, 1941. American and Filipino units await their fate with Homma moving against them from the north and pressure from advancing Japanese units near Baliuag.

THE JAPANESE DRIVE ON THE CENTRAL LUZON PLAIN

Homma's men push past the US defensive lines on their way to Manila

Note: Gridlines are shown at intervals of 10km/6.21 miles

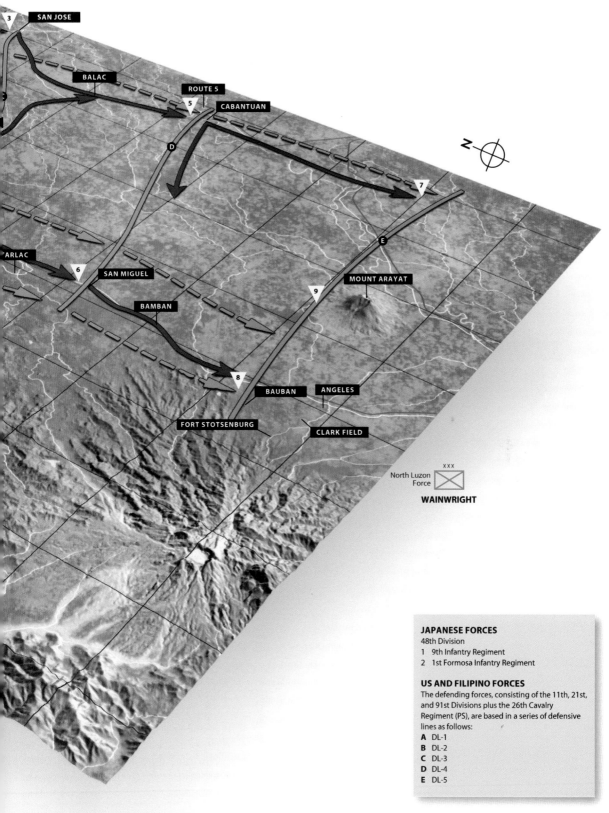

SAN JOSE

BALAC

ROUTE 5

CABANTUAN

5

D

ARLAC

6

SAN MIGUEL

BAMBAN

9

E

MOUNT ARAYAT

7

8

BAUBAN

ANGELES

FORT STOTSENBURG

CLARK FIELD

N

North Luzon
Force

XXX

WAINWRIGHT

JAPANESE FORCES
48th Division
1   9th Infantry Regiment
2   1st Formosa Infantry Regiment

US AND FILIPINO FORCES
The defending forces, consisting of the 11th, 21st,
and 91st Divisions plus the 26th Cavalry
Regiment (PS), are based in a series of defensive
lines as follows:
A   DL-1
B   DL-2
C   DL-3
D   DL-4
E   DL-5

American defenses had to rely on personnel like these grounded airmen, from the 17th Pursuit Squadron, to protect the service command area. These airmen, used as infantry, tried to push the Japanese soldiers out during the Battle of the Points. In the end trained infantry and tanks were needed. (US Air Force)

RIGHT
USAFFE soldiers conducted several successful defensive actions on Bataan. This occasionally led to the capture of IJA troops on the peninsula. Although weakened by a lack of supplies, the American-Filipino forces fought to the bitter end. (US Army)

Longoskawayan Point, the Navy had established an observation post on Mount Pucat to watch for any IJA movements to establish a beachhead leading to the Japanese control of Manila Bay's entrance. At 0840hrs on the morning of January 23, naval lookouts saw a force of about 300 Japanese soldiers moving inland from Longoskawayan Point. A combination of sailors, Marines, the 3rd Pursuit Squadron, the 301st Chemical Company, and a 2.95in. howitzer crew tried to dislodge the Japanese invaders. Thick jungle impeded their advance and this mixed force was facing battle-hardened Japanese infantry. The Americans managed to push back the Japanese, but could not defeat them.

The Japanese landing force came under intense artillery and mortar fire from American and Filipino positions, including 12in. mortars based on Corregidor. Despite this heavy fire and efforts to push the IJA soldiers off Longoskawayan Point, the provisional units still did not succeed in removing the Japanese and MacArthur had to send in trained infantry.

About 600 IJA troops consolidated at Quinauan Point despite the efforts of airmen from 34th Pursuit Squadron and a battalion of the 1st Philippine Constabulary to push them back. The IJA established a series of defensive positions while I Corps called for reinforcements and tanks to dislodge them. No tanks were available, since the American armor was engaged in supporting the withdrawal from the Abucay Line. Instead, the American-Filipino forces got two British Bren gun carriers and reinforcements from the 21st Pursuit Squadron, more Constabulary forces, and elements of the 71st Division. London had shipped the Bren gun carriers through the Philippines for Canadian forces defending Hong Kong, but they were stuck in Manila Bay.

The situation remained in the balance for several days while both the Japanese and Americans sought to reinforce their positions. Kimura committed his reserve battalion from Olongapo on the night of the 26/27th in an attempt to reinforce the Quinauan Point defenders. As with the earlier landings, the reinforcements came ashore at the wrong positions, at Anyasan Point north of Quinauan Point. When reports of these reinforcements were received by the Americans, Wainwright sent some units from the Philippine Division to reinforce the position on the evening of 27 January: the 3rd Battalion, 45th Infantry Regiment, moved against Quinauan Point, while the

2nd Battalion, 57th Infantry Regiment, went to the Longoskawayan Point. MacArthur also released some M3 tanks.

MacArthur made repeated calls for more aid from Washington. He still had a combined strength of about 90,000 troops on Bataan, Corregidor, and the outlaying coastal defense positions in Manila Bay, but the American-Filipino defenders had weakened on half-rations. Homma's forces had also sustained losses from combat, malaria, and the transfer of his best force, the 48th Division. Facing MacArthur was a depleted 65th Brigade and the Kimura Detachment, about 12,600 men. The remnants of the FEAF consisted of seven P-40s on Bataan. Despite their small numbers, FEAF pilots launched a daylight attack on their former bases at Neilson and Nichols Fields that caught Japanese aircraft on the ground, destroying several aircraft and raising the morale of MacArthur's forces.

Now reinforced by Philippine Scouts and tanks, the Americans and Filipinos made some progress and by January 29 the strengthened force destroyed the Japanese position on Longoskawayan Point. Wainwright's men used a combination of tanks, fire support from a minesweeper, artillery, and P-40s. At Quinauan Point, American and Filipino efforts to crush the Japanese took longer. The Philippine Scouts and Constabulary forces were not strong enough to push the Japanese back. Homma sent more reinforcements on the evening of February 1, but the remaining four FEAF P-40s, artillery, and PT boats attacked the amphibious force and sank half the force with the remnants going ashore at Canas Point.

Wainwright's troops at Quinauan Point used combined tank and infantry operations to press the Japanese who were located in a series of isolated pockets. Homma tried to evacuate his forces, but this largely failed with only 34 Japanese soldiers surviving the amphibious rescue attempt launched by the IJN. The Battle of the Points continued until February 13 as the last remaining pockets of IJA forces defied Wainwright's efforts to subdue them. MacArthur's men had thwarted the invasion and destroyed two of Homma's battalions.

HOMMA RETREATS NORTH

While the Battle of the Points played out, Homma's forces hammered the Bagac–Orion Line. With I and II Corps' retreat to the rear battle position the Japanese commanders tried to capitalize on the situation. Facing Wainwright, Homma sent in additional offensive forces by replacing Kimura with Lieutenant General Susumu Morioka, commander of the 16th Division, who brought in two additional infantry battalions and support units. Using night attacks all along the Bagac–Orion Line, the Japanese made some limited incursions.

Nara finally succeeded against II Corps when his forces breached the Bagac–Orion Line in two places on January 28. Against the thinly spread PA units, the Japanese punched through the line in the course of a night assault. One breach pushed some 400 yards into the line while the other penetrated about a mile. Despite these successes, Nara was not able to exploit them and the advance became bogged down. MacArthur's troops counterattacked, but they failed to defeat the Japanese and the situation degenerated into a stalemate. By February 8, Homma realized that he had to withdraw and he disengaged all along the Bagac–Orion Line and moved north. His forces required reinforcements and Homma requested reluctantly that the IGHQ send more forces.

DYESS TAKES AGLOLOMA BAY (pp. 70–71)

On February 8, 1942, Captain William "Ed" Dyess and 20 airmen who were being used as infantry landed near Agloloma Bay on the southern Bataan Peninsula, near Quinauan Point. Dyess' mission was to lead his meager forces to help evict Japanese units that had taken Quinauan Point. Dyess, who was commander of the 21st Pursuit Squadron, and his men embarked from Mariveles aboard two whaleboats towed by two modified 36ft gunboats. The gunboats had steel reinforced bows armed with 37mm antitank guns (1). American and Filipino forces had tied white bed sheets on trees near the top of the northern cliffs of the point to indicate positions where Japanese forces lay hidden in caves (2). American and Filipino soldiers and engineers had tried to eliminate these positions with dynamite, but some remained and it was Dyess's task to help root them out in America's first amphibious landing of the

war. The motor launches fired 37mm shells at the positions for ten minutes before the landings to suppress any enemy fire and the landing parties went ashore shortly after 0800hrs in a landing that was largely uncontested (3), apart from an aerial attack by three Mitsubishi K-30s (4). The Japanese eventually lost 600 men at Quinauan Point, while the Battle of the Points as a whole resulted in the destruction of two IJA battalions. Ed Dyess later helped sink a 12,000-ton transport and damage other ships at Subic Bay when in command of a P-40. Dyess survived the Bataan Death March and escaped Japanese imprisonment at Mindanao. An American submarine picked him up with other escapees and he provided one of the first accounts of the Bataan Death March. Dyess died in the course of a P-38 training flight in California in 1943.

IJN forces had to rely on heavy artillery, brought in from Malaya and other locations, to break through the Bagac–Orion Line on Bataan. Heavy Japanese artillery shelling and aerial bombing shattered the ebbing American and Filipino will and capability to fight. All the defenders could do was to wait for the Japanese offensive to begin and meet their eventual doom. (Tom Laemlein/Armor Plate Press)

The Japanese did launch a successful amphibious invasion against Mindoro, an island south of Luzon. One battalion landed unopposed on the northern end of the island, and although 50 Filipino soldiers protected the southern end of the island Homma's battalion did not engage them.

Homma's failure to conquer the Philippines, mounting casualties, and his request for more forces had embarrassed him in the IGHQ's eyes. The Japanese forces in the Philippines needed time to refit, recuperate, and reorganize. The 14th Army had sustained 2,700 killed and 4,000 wounded from early January to March 1 in Luzon, while as many as 12,000 Japanese soldiers suffered from disease and sickness. Homma was not capable of winning with a decimated division and a brigade. Reinforcements were not available in theater and the offensive was delayed. Active operations by IJA forces had begun against Singapore and the IJA still had the Netherlands East Indies to conquer.

The IGHQ approved more reinforcements to Homma on February 10, but Tokyo needed time to get the 4th Division from Shanghai to Bataan. IJA staff officers also sent additional siege artillery to break the Bagac–Orion Line. These units were based in Malaya and Hong Kong and moved quickly into position on Bataan. Homma could now hammer the American-Filipino forces with heavy artillery. Once the IJA conquered Bataan, this artillery could then turn its attention to Corregidor. Tokyo also allocated additional IJAAF and IJNAF bomber units to support the offensive. Since the movement and preparation of forces would take time, Homma hoped to launch operations by early April.

American and Filipino units celebrated the defense of the Bagac–Orion Line and some officers even advocated an offensive against Homma's forces to retake the Mauban–Abucay Line. However, higher morale could not overcome the lack of food and medicine and the defenders became weaker and more susceptible to diseases such beriberi, dysentery, and malaria. American-Filipino forces could only hope to dig in and stand fast.

MACARTHUR'S LAST STAND ON CORREGIDOR

MacArthur planned and directed operations from Corregidor. The island served as the main defensive position to protect Manila Bay, and Army engineers had built Fort Mills on Corregidor with 14 batteries to protect Manila Bay and Cavite. Fort Mills and other protected coastal defense positions could withstand naval and land-based artillery, but had little protection from the air strikes. With an assigned strength of 6,000 soldiers, the island was self-contained. It had a power plant, water desalination facility, a railroad, airfield, and housing. A key structure was the Malinta Tunnel, completed in 1932, which served as MacArthur's main headquarters during the campaign.

With an ever-tighter IJN blockade, the likelihood of reinforcement by surface shipping shrank with each passing day. Transports from Australia tried to reach Cebu where inter-island steamers could resupply Bataan and Corregidor, but only three out of six ships from Australia arrived in Cebu. The Japanese sank or captured most of the inter-island transportation, or the crews scuttled their ships. Roosevelt and Marshall continued their efforts to send men and material to MacArthur, the problem was a lack of naval resources to break the Japanese blockade. Submarines and aircraft did manage to resupply Bataan, but they could not provide all of the requirements. MacArthur blamed Roosevelt, Marshall, and the Navy for abandoning him.

Corregidor was the last major bastion of opposition in Luzon by the Americans and Filipinos. Japanese forces took a day to defeat the tired, starved defenders. This Japanese view of Corregidor's fall illustrates some of the conditions that the IJA invaders faced. The Japanese used only one of two planned amphibious landings to defeat the Americans. (US Army)

In Washington, Roosevelt and others started to realize that the Philippines fight was lost and that the USAFFE were on the cusp of defeat. MacArthur had held out against the Japanese and had attained a hero status in the eyes of the American public. Losing a major American possession, unlike Guam or Wake Island, was humiliating, but what might happen if Homma captured or killed MacArthur? Roosevelt ordered MacArthur to leave the Philippines and take command of forces in Australia and the Southwest Pacific Area on February 22, though he did not leave at once.

MacArthur left Corregidor on March 12, with his family and selected staff members departing in four PT boats for Mindanao. There, they flew by B-17 to Australia. Before he left, MacArthur made Wainwright the commander of all of the Luzon forces, although he planned to retain command of the USAFFE from Australia. MacArthur left Wainwright with the order to fight for as long as his troops had the ability to resist; no surrender was planned. However, this command relationship soon became confused.

LEFT
This photograph of Corregidor shows the eastern part of the island. The remnants of Kindley Field lie in the center, and at left center is Monkey Point, while opposite is Cavalry Point. The beach area to the lower right is where the Japanese landed during their invasion. (DOD)

RIGHT
This is one of the 4th Marine Regiment's beach defensive positions on Corregidor. The Japanese used heavy artillery and aerial bombardment to try to destroy these positions. (DOD)

BELOW
After Corregidor fell, Wainwright surrendered all forces in the Philippines fearing Japanese retribution if he did not capitulate. Some American commanders in the southern Philippines refused to surrender until ordered to do so. (US Army)

MacArthur reached Australia on 17 March. During a speech in Adelaide, he made a personal commitment to the Filipinos that he would return to the islands, declaring "I Shall Return." American officials tried to persuade him to change his statement to "We Shall Return," but he refused. His proclamation would serve as an American rallying cry and affect the entire future Pacific strategy. Japanese radio announcers labeled MacArthur as a deserter and coward for abandoning his men. To counter these claims, and because America needed a hero in the face of early defeats, Marshall convinced Roosevelt to nominate MacArthur for the Congressional Medal of Honor.

Both Roosevelt and Marshall had believed Wainwright had succeeded MacArthur as USAFFE commander and they arranged for Wainwright's promotion to lieutenant general. MacArthur tried to retain command of the USAFFE but Roosevelt and Marshall disagreed, and Marshall notified MacArthur that they considered Wainwright as the new commander of the US Forces in the Philippines (USFIP) on March 22. USFIP effectively replaced USAFFE and Wainwright named Major General Edward King as the commander of forces on Luzon.

THE FINAL ASSAULT AND FALL OF BATAAN

With MacArthur gone, no reinforcements, mounting casualties, and dwindling supplies, the morale of the American-Filipino defenders began to suffer. They knew that they were isolated and running out of supplies. By March 24, Homma's reinforcements were beginning to have an effect. IJA artillery battered the Bataan defenders, while IJAAF and IJNAF bombers struck targets on the peninsula. Japanese officers deployed added artillery along the southern edge of the eastern Bataan coastline and pounded the Manila Bay fortifications.

Time was on Homma's side. The IJA's 4th Division, with about 11,000 men, was to make the main effort to penetrate the line near Mount Samat. If successful, Homma's men would then push on to the southeast. Supporting this effort was the 65th Brigade. Divisionary attacks across the west coast of Bataan by elements of the 16th Division were intended to draw away and hold down enemy forces. The depleted, but rested 16th Division and 65th Brigade had each received about 3,500 replacements. Homma now estimated that the campaign would end in about a month.

Wainwright now had about 79,500 soldiers on Bataan, but most were sick or wounded. Dug-in PA units made up the great bulk of the forces. King used the remaining regiments of the Philippine Division and M3 tanks as his strategic reserve. Wainwright could call on concentrated artillery fire to hit the Japanese. However, much of the artillery lacked proper fire control, communications and transport – had to travel over rough ground, and had limited supplies of ammunition. Their targets also travelled in thick jungle that provided good cover against attack.

Japanese forces launched an attack against the Bagac–Orion Line at 0900hrs on April 3 with a massive artillery barrage. Homma hoped the six-hour barrage would smash American defensive positions and artillery batteries. After the barrage, the Japanese then concentrated their artillery and air attacks against the 41st Division holding the area near Mount Samat. This was the center of the line and the weakest point of the defenses, just as in the Abucay–Mauban Line. In one day, the Japanese badly mauled the 41st Division. By 1500hrs, the Japanese had skillfully maneuvered around the defenses created by the Filipinos and were advancing south against minimal opposition. Barbed wire, fortifications, mines, and strongpoints slowed, but failed to stop the 4th Division.

Over the next few days, the Japanese pushed back the PA units in Mount Samat area. Despite counterattacks and the use of reserves, King's men could not regain the original main line of resistance. The line with II Corps units began to fall apart under intensified air attacks, artillery, and pressure by Homma's troops. The Americans and Filipinos continued to retreat south all along the peninsula. By April 8, Homma's staff had received accounts that PA units had started to retreat to Cabcaben and Mariveles. Coastal artillery units and other reserves, originally assigned to defend the beaches, were now in the line fighting the advancing Japanese. Homma also learned from air reconnaissance that boats had arrived in Mariveles, Cabcaben, and all along the east coast. This could indicate King's men would start moving to Corregidor and escape capture. If Homma struck hard now, then he might capture the entire force.

Homma devised a scheme to move his 4th Division through the foothills and take Mariveles. The 16th Division would follow down the East Road and harass the enemy all the way to Mariveles. Nara's 65th Brigade was to drive west to cut off I Corps. On April 9, Homma's troops executed the plan and the operation was easier than he expected. The weakened, demoralized defenders could not halt the Japanese tanks and they reached Mariveles by 1300hrs on the first day of the offensive. King had realized that with II Corps disintegrating and no way to reinforce his forces Bataan was lost. At 0330hrs, he sought out the Japanese lines to capitulate. By 1230hrs, King had surrendered and Bataan had fallen.

THE BATAAN DEATH MARCH

One of the most infamous actions in World War II occurred soon after King surrendered Bataan. Japanese guards killed and maimed thousands of prisoners of war and civilians in the course of the "Bataan Death March." The fall of Bataan meant thousands of wounded and malnourished prisoners fell into Homma's hands. Homma's staff had planned for only 25,000 captives, but the Japanese took about 78,000 prisoners (12,000 American and 60,000–70,000 Filipino) on Bataan. With limited transportation available, Homma could only force the Americans and Filipinos to walk out of the peninsula to prison camps, and the Japanese marched prisoners 65 miles to Camp O'Donnell in central Luzon.

Conditions on the forced march were abysmal for the prisoners. Given no food, water, or medical aid, the prisoners had to deal with overbearing heat, their own poor health, and the brutal guards. IJA soldiers did not give their prisoners any relief, beating or killing any stragglers that fell behind. Under the Japanese *Bushido* warrior code, surrender was abhorrent since a soldier's duty was to fight to the death. If a soldier gave up, then he forfeited the right to humane treatment – in contrast the Americans and Filipinos had surrendered en masse. Any civilian offering aid to the prisoners also faced severe punishment or death. The Japanese guards and harsh conditions killed about 2,330 Americans and 7,000 to 10,000 Filipinos during the march. This was the only start of over three years of mistreatment for these prisoners. Many American prisoners would move to China, Formosa, and Japan to labor and die for Imperial Japan.

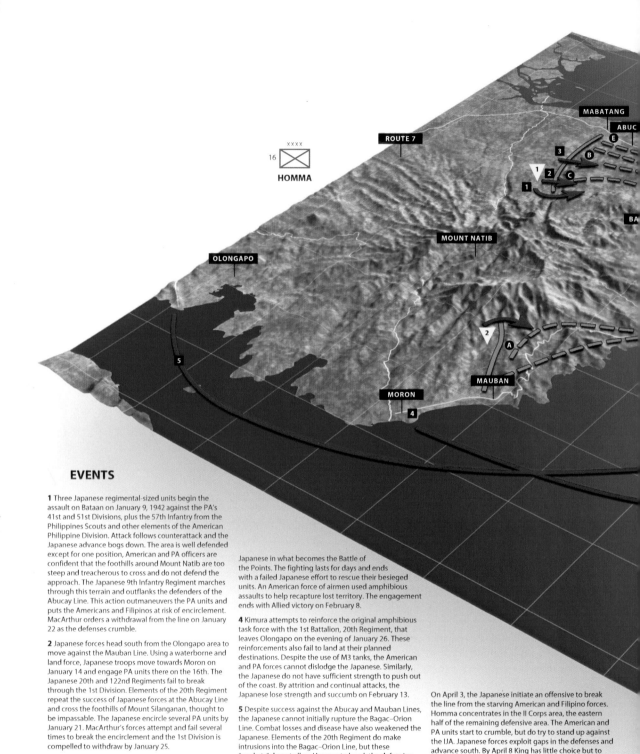

MABATANG

ABUC

E

ROUTE 7

3 B

16 ⊠

HOMMA

1 · 2 · C

1

BA

MOUNT NATIB

OLONGAPO

2

A

MAUBAN

5

MORON

4

EVENTS

1 Three Japanese regimental-sized units begin the assault on Bataan on January 9, 1942 against the PA's 41st and 51st Divisions, plus the 57th Infantry from the Philippines Scouts and other elements of the American Philippine Division. Attack follows counterattack and the Japanese advance bogs down. The area is well defended except for one position, American and PA officers are confident that the foothills around Mount Natib are too steep and treacherous to cross and do not defend the approach. The Japanese 9th Infantry Regiment marches through this terrain and outflanks the defenders of the Abucay Line. This action outmaneuvers the PA units and puts the Americans and Filipinos at risk of encirclement. MacArthur orders a withdrawal from the line on January 22 as the defenses crumble.

2 Japanese forces head south from the Olongapo area to move against the Mauban Line. Using a waterborne and land force, Japanese troops move towards Moron on January 14 and engage PA units there on the 16th. The Japanese 20th and 122nd Regiments fail to break through the 1st Division. Elements of the 20th Regiment repeat the success of Japanese forces at the Abucay Line and cross the foothills of Mount Silanganan, thought to be impassable. The Japanese encircle several PA units by January 21. MacArthur's forces attempt and fail several times to break the encirclement and the 1st Division is compelled to withdraw by January 25.

3 In an attempt to create havoc in the enemy's rear, Homma directs the 2nd Battalion, 20th Regiment, to land behind the Bagac–Orion Line. Japanese landing craft move infantry to the Caibobo Point area on the night of January 22, but they land well south of this target at two areas. American and PA reserves fight the

Japanese in what becomes the Battle of the Points. The fighting lasts for days and ends with a failed Japanese effort to rescue their besieged units. An American force of airmen used amphibious assaults to help recapture lost territory. The engagement ends with Allied victory on February 8.

4 Kimura attempts to reinforce the original amphibious task force with the 1st Battalion, 20th Regiment, that leaves Olongapo on the evening of January 26. These reinforcements also fail to land at their planned destinations. Despite the use of M3 tanks, the American and PA forces cannot dislodge the Japanese. Similarly, the Japanese do not have sufficient strength to push out of the coast. By attrition and continual attacks, the Japanese lose strength and succumb on February 13.

5 Despite success against the Abucay and Mauban Lines, the Japanese cannot initially rupture the Bagac–Orion Line. Combat losses and disease have also weakened the Japanese. Elements of the 20th Regiment do make intrusions into the Bagac–Orion Line, but these "pockets" do not allow Homma to break the defensive positions in late January. Homma must now ask for additional reinforcements and he withdraws from the line. This provides a valuable respite for MacArthur. With additional forces, including artillery and bombers, Homma prepares for an attack with renewed strength. Artillery and aerial bombardments start on March 24.

On April 3, the Japanese initiate an offensive to break the line from the starving American and Filipino forces. Homma concentrates in the II Corps area, the eastern half of the remaining defensive area. The American and PA units start to crumble, but do try to stand up against the IJA. Japanese forces exploit gaps in the defenses and advance south. By April 8 King has little choice but to surrender the Luzon Force. Prisoners begin their trek in the infamous Bataan Death March to San Fernando.

6 The Japanese take Mariveles on April 9 and effectively encircle the remaining I Corps forces. With Bataan taken, Homma can now concentrate on Corregidor at the base of the peninsula.

THE FALL OF BATAAN, JANUARY 9–APRIL 9, 1942

The major US and Filipino effort to defend the Bataan Peninsula against the Japanese.

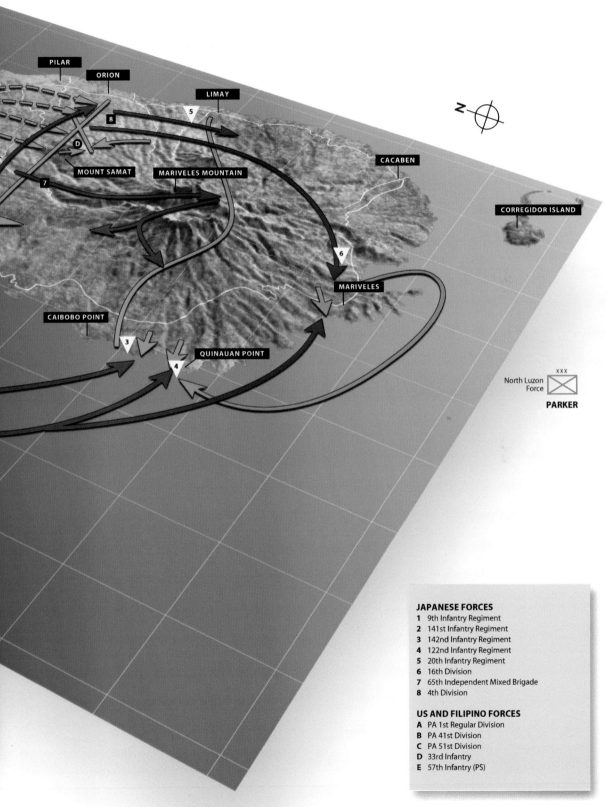

PILAR

ORION

LIMAY

8

5

D

7

MOUNT SAMAT

MARIVELES MOUNTAIN

CACABEN

CORREGIDOR ISLAND

6

MARIVELES

CAIBOBO POINT

3

4

QUINAUAN POINT

North Luzon Force

xxx

PARKER

N

JAPANESE FORCES
1   9th Infantry Regiment
2   141st Infantry Regiment
3   142nd Infantry Regiment
4   122nd Infantry Regiment
5   20th Infantry Regiment
6   16th Division
7   65th Independent Mixed Brigade
8   4th Division

US AND FILIPINO FORCES
A   PA 1st Regular Division
B   PA 41st Division
C   PA 51st Division
D   33rd Infantry
E   57th Infantry (PS)

CORREGIDOR FALLS

With Bataan's fall, Corregidor was next in line. The American-Filipino forces on the island were isolated, but Homma still required time to prepare for an amphibious operation to take the island. To break down the defenders, the Japanese intensified their air and artillery bombardments.

These attacks left facilities on Corregidor heavily damaged and it became increasingly difficult to prepare the defenses on the island. Coastal defense artillery designed to ward off a naval attack could do little to thwart an amphibious invasion from Bataan. The American garrison consisted of some 11,611 American and Filipino military personnel, with the 4th Marine Regiment and others providing much of the beach defenses with 1,514 personnel. As survivors from Bataan arrived, the numbers increased to some 4,000 men protecting the beaches.

Heavy pre-invasion artillery and air attacks hit Corregidor starting on April 29. These attacks started to shatter the defenders, and Japanese commanders planned to launch two landings with a regiment apiece. The first landing, scheduled for May 5, was to take place on the north coast at Infantry Point. The 4th Division's 61th Infantry Regiment, with tanks, would take Malinta Hill and its tunnel. The next day, the 37th Infantry Regiment and other reinforcements would come ashore between Morrison and Battery Points at 2330hrs to complete the assault. Homma could not land both regiments at the same time owing to the lack of landing craft.

Homma's artillery had fired 16,000 rounds against Corregidor on May 4, pounding the island with shells up to 240mm in diameter. The artillery and bomber attacks had now obliterated most of the beach defenses and surface facilities, causing some 600 casualties. On May 4 Wainwright radioed Marshall that he had "less than an even chance to beat off an assault."

Also on May 4, sound detectors on the island indicated vessels approaching Corregidor at 2100hrs. By 2200hrs, the defenders saw the landing craft getting close to the island and the Japanese came ashore about 1,000 yards east of the planned invasion site due to tides. Heavy fire by two 75mm guns ripped into the invaders and Homma reportedly lost two-thirds of the force and 31 vessels. The second invasion force could not launch from Bataan because of these losses. Although the IJA suffered heavy losses, it advanced despite resistance by Marines at the beach. Japanese soldiers captured the Denver Battery, but the Americans fought on.

A provisional battalion of 500 sailors, soldiers, and Marines launched a counterattack at 0600hrs, but the Americans and Filipinos could not stop the Japanese and they started to fall back towards the Malinta Tunnel. IJA soldiers had infiltrated the American defenses and Homma's men, along with three tanks, had killed about 600 to 800 defenders and wounded 1,000 more. By 1000hrs Wainwright decided to surrender Corregidor as he had no way of stopping the Japanese armor. Homma's men took the Malinta Tunnel and by 1100hrs all of the hostilities ended, at least on Corregidor. Wainwright ordered a ceasefire to prevent a slaughter and sought out the Japanese to surrender.

SOUTHERN PHILIPPINES OPERATIONS

While Homma struggled against the American-Filipino force on Bataan he did not neglect Mindanao and other areas south of Luzon. With his limited forces, Homma had to request reinforcements to take the rest of the Philippines, especially Mindanao. The IGHQ sent elements of the 18th Division, 5th Division (from Malaya), and other units to the 14th Army to conclude the Philippines campaign.

The first move in the south was against the Visayan Islands between Mindanao and Luzon. MacArthur had assigned five PA divisions to the area, but he had redeployed almost two divisions to help defend Luzon. This command was thinly spread in static defenses, and the most serious problem was the lack of artillery support. Many units had few trained personnel and most soldiers lacked even the most basic equipment, such as steel helmets.

Brigadier General Bradford Chynoweth commanded the Visayan area with 20,000 men. The most important IJA targets were the Cebu and Panay Islands. PA units did have time to construct some defensive positions throughout the islands, but trying to protect them against a mobile foe with poorly trained and equipped forces appeared to be an impossible task. The first sign of Japanese moves in this area was on April 9 when Chynoweth received reports that an IJN invasion force of 4,852 troops was headed for Cebu. Major General Kiyotake Kawaguchi, the 35th Brigade commander from the 18th Division, plus support forces landed on Cebu's east and west coasts. Chynoweth had about 6,500 men to face him.

The main city of Cebu fell in a day. PA units tried to defend Cantabaco, which controlled the only cross-island road but failed to hang on. This action signaled the end of Chynoweth's control of Cebu. Chynoweth moved north to organize a guerilla movement on April 12, eventually surrendering a month later.

RIGHT
The Malinta Tunnel consisted of a warren of passages. It had four entrances with lateral passages that contained storage areas, shelters, maintenance shops, and headquarters. Unfortunately, aircraft and artillery bombardments damaged its power plant. This reduced lighting and ventilation and created harsh living conditions. (Department of Defense)

LEFT
This photograph shows the crowded conditions that soldiers endured in the Malinta Tunnel during the campaign. Conditions deteriorated throughout the campaign until the invasion of Corregidor on May 5. (US Army)

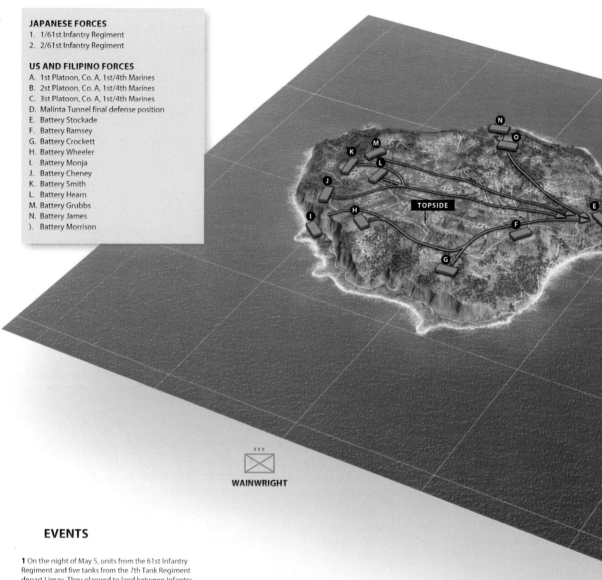

JAPANESE FORCES
1. 1/61st Infantry Regiment
2. 2/61st Infantry Regiment

US AND FILIPINO FORCES
A. 1st Platoon, Co. A, 1st/4th Marines
B. 2st Platoon, Co. A, 1st/4th Marines
C. 3st Platoon, Co. A, 1st/4th Marines
D. Malinta Tunnel final defense position
E. Battery Stockade
F. Battery Ramsey
G. Battery Crockett
H. Battery Wheeler
I. Battery Monja
J. Battery Cheney
K. Battery Smith
L. Battery Hearn
M. Battery Grubbs
N. Battery James
). Battery Morrison

TOPSIDE

WAINWRIGHT

EVENTS

1 On the night of May 5, units from the 61st Infantry Regiment and five tanks from the 7th Tank Regiment depart Limay. They planned to land between Infantry Point and North Point at 2300hrs. The 1st Battalion, 61st Infantry, (approximately 790 men commanded by Colonel Gempachi Sato) lands at 2315hrs. However, the 2nd Battalion hits the beach to the east of its intended landing site due to strong tides. Marine defenders sink eight of the ten landing craft with machine guns, a 75mm gun battery, and 37mm guns. Many Japanese officers and men are killed.

2 Sato's men must take Corregidor alone. The few American defenders on Corregidor's "tail" are inadequate to hold their positions. Marines defending the "tail" of Corregidor Island start advance towards Battery Denver. Sato had advanced towards Monkey Point and Battery Denver. His men capture Monkey Point at 0100hrs May 6. The Japanese also move to Battery Denver at 2350hrs and take it 0130hrs. Marines and other forces attempt to counterattack, but fail to dislodge Sato's men who are digging in. The Japanese consolidate their position with men from the 2nd Battalion and the Americans move up more troops from gun batteries and other positions to attack Sato.

3 At 0600hrs, American units counterattack and succeed in pushing back the Japanese. However, the Americans cannot exploit their success. Japanese soldiers had infiltrated American lines and now operate light artillery from the island against the defenders. Using three tanks that landed (two Type 97s and one M3), Sato begins an advance about 1000hrs. Japanese forces rake the Americans with heavy machine-gun fire and artillery. American casualties mount and they must retreat.

4 American forces fall back towards Malinta Hill and they establish a new defensive line. The Americans have few means to resist and no way to stop the Japanese armor. Wainwright feared that he could not stop another Japanese landing. He believed a slaughter of his men would ensue. His decision to surrender is made at 1000hrs. Wainwright orders that a radio message be sent to the Japanese that all resistance will end as of 1200hrs. He also orders the destruction of weapons above .45-cal. to ensure the Japanese cannot use the coastal defense artillery and other arms.

HOMMA TAKES CORREGIDOR, MAY 5–6, 1942

The last major bastion of American and Filipino resistance on Luzon is overrun by Japanese amphibious forces.

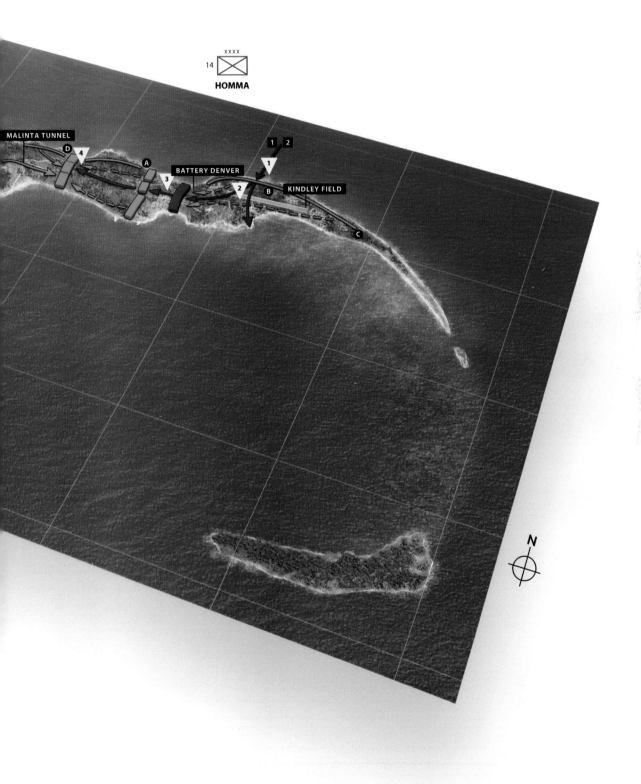

xxxx

14 HOMMA

MALINTA TUNNEL

D 4

A

BATTERY DENVER

3

1 2

1

2

B

KINDLEY FIELD

C

N

On April 16, Homma sent a brigade-sized force of 4,160 men, the Kawamura Detachment, to take Panay. Like Cebu, the American-Filipino force tried to delay the Japanese through the demolition of bridges and roads. The 61st Division, with over 7,000 personnel, was then to retreat north to conduct guerilla warfare. The Kawamura Detachment landed unopposed and they soon controlled major roads and towns. Although some guerilla activity occurred, the IJA controlled all of Panay by April 20.

Mindanao was next. IJA forces had earlier taken Davao and Digos, but had not expanded their beachhead. Homma's plan was to launch two amphibious invasions by the Kawamura and Kawaguchi Detachments. From Digos, Japanese forces would drive north to link up with the invading forces. From Cebu, the Kawaguchi Detachment landed in the west near Parang on April 29 with 4,852 men. Despite opposition by the 101st and parts of the 1st Regular Divisions, the Japanese succeeded in landing. With air and artillery support, the IJA slowly moved towards Mindanao's center. The Kawamura Detachment, landed near Cagayan and Togoloan, close to Del Monte Field, on May 3.

These Japanese soldiers inspect coastal defense artillery positions on Corregidor. The Americans operated a number of "disappearing" guns protected behind massive fortifications to shield them from naval gunfire, though they did not have protection from aerial attack. The largest caliber disappearing guns at Corregidor had 12in.-diameter barrels. The defenders of Corregidor also operated 12in. mortars, antiaircraft guns, and other weapons. (Tom Laemlein/Armor Plate Press)

With invasion by the Kawamura Detachment, the American control of Mindanao was tenuous. Sharp, commanding Mindanao, ordered a general withdrawal to the center of the island as the Japanese started to push into the more mountainous areas. The Japanese offensive had slowed near Dalig, east of Del Monte, but by May 9 the IJA had routed Sharp's forces and the fight was over.

Japanese invading forces captured thousands of American and Filipino soldiers on Corregidor. Here survivors leave the Malinta Tunnel. Although the tunnel withstood heavy bombardment, it could not hold out against ground attacks. (US Air Force)

The fall of Mindanao

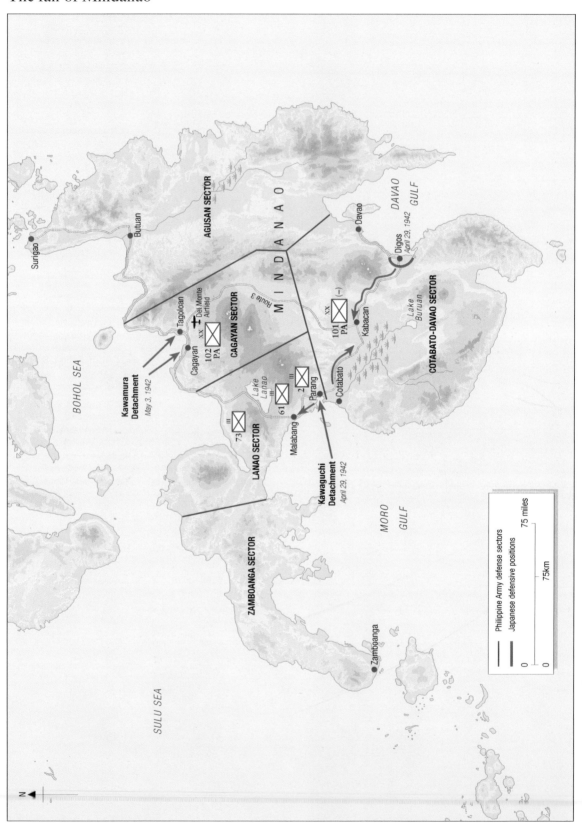

FINAL SURRENDER

Homma had been perplexed when King surrendered Bataan to the Japanese. The 14th Army commander had believed that all forces had capitulated. Instead, Homma had to fight against Corregidor and the southern Philippines. Just before Corregidor's fall, Wainwright had released his command of the Mindanao-Visayan forces to Sharp on May 6. However, Homma would not accept Wainwright's surrender unless all American-Filipino forces gave up. Fearing retaliation against his vulnerable men on Corregidor, Wainwright ordered all American and Filipino forces to surrender via a radio broadcast from Manila on May 7.

Meanwhile, MacArthur had directed Sharp to disregard Wainwright's order to surrender. MacArthur believed Wainwright had become "temporarily unbalanced." Wainwright had to remove Sharp as commander and then order him to surrender his Mindanao-Visayan forces. In the Visayan Islands, some American officers still in command after their troops and also disagreed with Wainwright's decision. Instead of giving up, these forces escaped into the jungles where they conducted a long guerilla struggle. Other pockets of resistance on Luzon did the same, but organized resistance had ceased by June 9, about six months after the start of the campaign.

Despite putting up a tough fight, American and Filipino forces succumbed to overwhelming Japanese superiority. This scene was repeated on Bataan, Corregidor, Mindanao, and other islands in the archipelago. (Tom Laemlein/Armor Plate Press)

AFTERMATH

The Philippines campaign provided many valuable lessons for Washington. Pre-war Pacific strategy did not reflect the resources or situation facing the United States in 1942. The Japanese attack demonstrated how unprepared America was for a global war. Even if he had possessed a trained PA and sufficient resources, MacArthur was isolated in the Philippines and Japanese forces would have taken the archipelago eventually. The islands' defenders did slow the Japanese planned 50-day campaign to about six months, but this did not alter events in the Pacific appreciably as the Japanese still took control of Southeast Asia, and although Tokyo had to commit additional resources to the Philippines, this was a relatively small price to pay for a valuable prize. Though little positive for the Americans came out of the early days of the Pacific, the American-Filipino defiance proved that the Japanese were not supermen and that a determined effort could stop them. The defense of Bataan and Corregidor provided a glimmer of hope while news of the Bataan Death March galvanized the public's continued support for the struggle against Japan. Given the proper leadership and equipment, the American Army had met the Japanese and, in some cases, bested them. MacArthur also became a symbol to America, a hero.

The Philippines campaign illustrated that Washington needed to take further steps to face Japan and Germany in combat. Training, command and control, equipment, joint planning, and communications systems all needed great improvements to beat the Axis powers. The United States faced a long road to improve its military capabilities. Fortunately, the US economy was still in the early stages of full mobilization while both the Army and Navy were also building up their forces through a greatly expanded training program

The Philippines defense faced many challenges. The strategy to hold the Philippines until assistance could come from the continental US was admirable, but the destruction of much of the Pacific Fleet undid WPO-3. The loss of the fleet ensured the Philippines' demise. Without sufficient logistics, the American-Filipino force was lost. The lack of coordinated command and control between the Army and Navy in the Philippines did not help as MacArthur and Hart fought separate campaigns. MacArthur considered WPO-3 and the Navy's plan to move south as unsound and he developed a separate plan for a more active defense. At one stroke MacArthur abandoned years of training and preparations for WPO-3 with this modification. The Philippines' defenses suffered without a single commander and control of overall strategy became a point of major contention. The Joint

American forces in the Pacific became masters of amphibious operations on a grand scale. MacArthur fervently hoped to return to the Philippines, which he did in late 1944 supported by a massive display of American naval and air power. (DOD)

Army and Navy Planning Board was a step towards improved planning and strategy, but Roosevelt needed more. Fortunately, during the ARCADIA conference, Roosevelt and Churchill agreed on the formation of the Combined Chiefs of Staff to develop grand strategy. At the same time the US created the Joint Chiefs of Staff on which Roosevelt relied for the highest level of military advice regarding strategy, planning, and operations. This body was successful throughout World War II and still operates today.

The scene was set for the defeat of MacArthur's forces early in the campaign. The destruction of the FEAF bombers and fighters after a single day of combat unraveled all efforts to defend the islands. The unexplained loss of many B-17s and other FEAF aircraft following hours of warning was inexcusable. To this day, no one knows who was responsible for the loss of these aircraft. Air power could have helped defend the Philippines and support efforts to resupply the defenders. As at Pearl Harbor, the Philippines campaign demonstrated the value of the airplane to the American military. Japanese air superiority allowed Homma to conduct operations without FEAF opposition and to bomb at will.

MacArthur's strategy of attempting to defend the entire Philippines, instead of implementing WPO-3, forced him to base his forces throughout Luzon and the southern Philippines. His belief that the terrain of the Philippines along with his PA divisions would stop the Japanese was deluded. He underestimated the IJA's ability to fight. Instead of concentrating his forces in Bataan, MacArthur laid his forces out to be defeated piecemeal. The dispersal of forces also meant that American officers had to struggle to supply and equip widely deployed units rather than building up reserves in Bataan. MacArthur's strategy of active defense also reduced the time available for the construction of defensive positions in Bataan. Improved logistics may not have saved Bataan, but it could have strengthened military capabilities and reduced the suffering of the American-Filipino defenders.

The primary role assigned to PA units, who were not front-line soldiers, was nothing more than a fanciful hope on MacArthur's part. MacArthur had assumed that his soldiers would defeat any invader at their most vulnerable position on the beaches. Instead of using his best-trained and equipped Philippine Division and the PA 1st Regular Division, he kept most of these troops in reserve and away from the fighting until Bataan. The defense of the isolated Visayan Islands and Mindanao also forced MacArthur to distribute his forces to outlying areas instead of concentrating them on Luzon. The campaign also highlighted the Americans' underestimation of Japanese military capabilities, especially the IGHQ's ability to wage near-simultaneous campaigns separated by thousands of miles.

This being said, MacArthur faced almost insurmountable odds. Against a strong Japanese military threat and at a great distance from America, the USAFFE had little chance of mounting a successful, long-term defense. Some in Washington believed in WPO-3 and a possible reinforcement of the Philippines. In reality, Washington could either build-up its garrison or retreat once war started. It decided to try to reinforce its forces despite the strategic focus of Germany first, and Roosevelt and Marshall could not meet the massive aid and reinforcements demanded by MacArthur. The Pacific Fleet's losses, limited available resources, and commitments to Europe made the defense of the Philippines questionable. The American-Filipino force could only hope to surrender or face a total defeat. Still, with MacArthur's presence in Australia and the Navy's beating in the Pacific, military leaders conducted a heated debate about the agreed upon "Germany first" strategy. MacArthur and Chief of Naval Operations, Admiral Ernest King, fought the decision made by Roosevelt and Churchill, and pushed for more and better forces in the Pacific to stem Japanese advances towards Australia and the Netherlands East Indies. In this they were partly successful.

The Army had 1,644,000 personnel in uniform on December 7, 1941. Most were still undergoing training, but limited forces were available for deployment overseas. Despite the call for "Germany first", the immediate

THE FIGHTING FILIPINOS
WE WILL ALWAYS FIGHT FOR *FREEDOM!*

threat in the Pacific drew the majority of Army and Navy forces into the Pacific in early 1942. The War Department sent five of its eight deployable divisions to the Pacific, along with two Army divisions in Hawaii and a Marine Corps division in New Zealand. The United States had a sizable force to try to thwart the Japanese advance into Borneo and New Guinea. The AAF sent 1,300 aircraft to the region, which represented about 60 percent of its entire force.

Homma did have initial success in the Philippines. Gaining air superiority and defeating the American-Filipino forces on the ground provided great examples of the Japanese operational and tactical prowess to the world. The IJA and IJN had demonstrated its military capabilities, but it was largely against an untrained PA force with few supplies. Defeat of the Americans was sweet, but there were major problems. Homma and the IGHQ misidentified the center of gravity for MacArthur. Japanese officers assumed that the fall of Manila would compel MacArthur to capitulate. Instead, the center of gravity was the American-Filipino force on Bataan which continued to resist and upset Homma's plans. The premature transfer of the 48th Division to aid the IJA efforts in Malaya significantly reduced Homma's ability to defeat a much larger, albeit weak and mostly untrained, enemy. Fortunately, for Homma, the American-Filipino force did not have the resources to mount the kind of major counterattack that could have reversed his gains in Bataan. The IGHQ assumed MacArthur's position was hopeless, and continued with the division's withdrawal, thus making a strategic miscalculation. Homma still defeated the Americans in sustained battle and the Japanese could focus on building its Greater East Asia Co-prosperity Sphere. The Philippines allowed Tokyo to accomplish its pre-war goal of seizing resource-rich Southeast Asia, but it was not cheap.

Like Washington, Tokyo had to defend the Philippines later in the war because of its strategic position. Loss of the Philippines would lead to a threat to its lines of communications and transportation for its raw materials from

Southeast Asia, the major reason it went to war in the first place. Additionally, it served as a perceived jumping-off point for the Americans to strike the Japanese homeland. Finally, with the numerous Japanese garrisons in the area the Philippines' recapture would isolate those forces in Malaya and surrounding territories. The IGHQ would have to conduct a massive defensive effort to retain the Philippines if Washington allowed MacArthur to keep his promise to return.

The Japanese also confirmed, something already heralded by its behavior in China, that their espoused focus on releasing Asian-Pacific peoples from the yoke of colonial oppression was just an illusion. The Bataan Death March and the brutal occupation in the Philippines showed the true colors of Japanese aims – total domination of the Far East, not the "freeing" of oppressed Asian people. Instead of gaining the status of liberator, the IJA and IJN became oppressors with the result that bands of guerillas fought the Japanese until the Americans returned.

On October 20, 1944, MacArthur returned to the Philippines with the invasion of Leyte. The recapture of the Philippines saw guerillas, major naval operations, kamikaze attacks on the American fleet, tough urban fighting in Manila, jungle fighting, and Japanese atrocities. By May 1945 the majority of Japanese organized resistance had ended. The Philippines, along with Iwo Jima and Okinawa, demonstrated how tough the Japanese military could fight when they were cornered, a dubious omen for the planned invasion of Japan.

The fall of the Philippines was a humiliating defeat for Washington. It was the largest single surrender of American forces in military history and eliminated Washington's forward presence in the Far East. It meant years of suffering for the conquered Philippine people and American prisoners, though the exploits on Bataan and Corregidor rallied the American public for the long struggle ahead. The Philippines campaign and later promises to liberate the islands showed that Washington would not abandon the Filipinos. MacArthur's rise as a national hero also meant that he would put his stamp on grand strategy that helped create separate lines of advance for the Americans through the Southwest and Central Pacific.

THE BATTLEFIELDS TODAY

Time, natural events, war, and economic development have changed the face of the Philippines since 1942. Manila and other cities may have been largely untouched in the fighting of 1941 and 1942, but suffered great physical destruction in the campaigns to liberate the islands in 1944 and 1945. The two major US military facilities, Clark Air Force Base and Subic Naval Base, reverted back to Philippine control after their leases expired in the early 1990s, and the explosion of Mount Pinatubo on June 15, 1991, produced a tremendous volcanic event that caused great physical damage to Clark Air Force Base where hangars and facilities collapsed. However, despite the changes key areas in the campaign to invade the Philippines still remain.

There are several locations that visitors can see around Luzon. Many of the beaches around the island remain undeveloped. Visits to the Lingayen Gulf and Lamon Bay area can easily be made via automobile from Manila. One can view the beaches and Japanese advance routes towards Manila. The Bataan Peninsula also has areas worth visiting. Visitors can trace the Bataan Death March from the peninsula route to the Capas National Shrine in Tarlac, near Camp O'Donnell. One can also observe locations where the Battle of the Points occurred.

One particular site, Corregidor, is well worth the one-hour ferry ride from Manila. Guided tours take tourists for a day trip or one can stay overnight. Visitors can explore the Malinta Tunnel, Topside facilities, coastal defensive artillery gun emplacements, and the Japanese invasion sites located on the "tail" of Corregidor. The island also has several memorials to the American and Filipino soldiers who defended it and died at their posts.

BIBLIOGRAPHY

Caiden, Marin, *The Ragged, Rugged Warriors* New York: Ballantine Books, 1966

Coffman, Edward, *The Regulars: The American Army 1898–1941* Cambridge, MA: Belknap Press of Harvard University Press, 2004

Connaughton, Richard, *MacArthur and Defeat in the Philippines* Woodstock, NY: Overlook, 2001

Cravens, Wesley, and Cate, James, *The Army Air Forces in World War II, Volume One, Plans and Early Operations January 1939 to August 1942* Chicago, IL: The University of Chicago Press, 1948

Dull, Paul, *A Battle History of the Imperial Japanese Navy (1941–1945)* Annapolis, MD: Naval Institute Press, 1978

Hogg, Ian, *Great Land Battles of World War II* Garden City, NY: Doubleday, 1987

Kennedy, Paul, *Pacific Onslaught* New York: Ballantine Books, 1972

Linn, Brian, *Guardians of Empire: The US Army and the Pacific 1902–1940* Chapel Hills, NC: University of North Caroline Press, 1997

Matloff, Maurice, and Snell, Edwin, *Strategic Planning for Coalition Warfare, 1941–1942* Washington, DC: Center of Military History, 1999

Miller, Edward, *War Plan Orange: The US Strategy to Defeat Japan, 1897–1945* Annapolis, MD: Naval Institute Press, 1991

Mortensen, Daniel, "Delaying Action or Foul Deception" in Bernard Nalty (ed.) *Pearl Harbor and the War in the Pacific* New York: Smithmark, 1991

Morton, Louis, *The Fall of the Philippines* Washington, DC: Center of Military History, 1989

——, "The Decision to Withdraw to Bataan" in Kent Greenfield (ed.) *Command Decisions* Washington, DC: Center of Military History, 2000

——, *Strategy and Command: The First Two Years* Washington, DC: Center of Military History, 1962

Nalty, Bernard, et al., *With Courage: The US Army Air Forces in World War II* Washington, DC: Air Force History & Museums Program, 1994

Perret, Geoffrey, *Old Soldiers Never Die: The Life of Douglas MacArthur* New York: Random House, 1996

——, *Winged Victory* New York: Random House, 1993

Shimada, Koichi "Air Operations in the Philippines" in D. C. Evans (ed.) *The Japanese Navy in World War II* Annapolis, MD: Naval Institute Press, 1971

Spector, Ronald, *Eagle Against the Sun: The American War with Japan* New York: Vintage Books, 1985

Sugita, Ichiji "Conquest of the Philippines" Compiled from Japanese Demobilization Bureau Records in *Reports of General MacArthur Japanese Operations in the Southwest Pacific Area Volume II-Part I* Washington, DC: Center of Military History, 1994

Toland, John, *The Rising Sun* New York: Random House, 1970